CU00836005

QUOTABLE POLITICIANS

Quotable

POLITICIANS

by
Carole McKenzie

MAINSTREAM
PUBLISHING
EDINBURGH AND LONDON

First published in Great Britain in 1995 by
MAINSTREAM PUBLISHING COMPANY
(EDINBURGH) LTD
7 Albany Street
Edinburgh EH1 3UG

ISBN 1 85158 652 0

Illustrations by Carolyn Ridsdale

A catalogue record for this book is available from the
British Library

Typeset in Sabon by Litho Link Ltd, Welshpool, Powys
Printed in Finland by WSOY

For John,
a politician of many talents.
'ETHICS – the soul of integrity.'

A C H I E V E M E N T

This is the greatest week in the history of the world since the creation.
Richard Nixon (1913-94) on the first human landing on the moon

Edwina Currie is to the Conservative Party what the Bishop of Durham is to the Church of England.
Richard Holt

A C T I O N

A man who has to be convinced to act before he acts is not a man of action.
George Clemenceau (1841-1929), French statesman

So here is a pretty fly out of the King of the Netherlands! Who has bit him I cannot guess: we have some suspicion of France.
Lord Palmerston (1784-1865) British statesman, commenting on the French invasion of Belgium, 1831

I don't mind your being killed, but I object to your being taken prisoner.
Lord Kitchener (1850-1916), British statesman to Edward VIII (then Prince of Wales) when requesting to go to the Front, 1914

Better to enjoy and suffer than sit around with folded arms. You know the only true prayer? Please God, lead me into temptation.
Jennie Lee (1904-88), Labour politician and wife of Aneurin Bevan

When the President says 'Jump' they only ask, 'How high?'
John Ehrlichman, Assistant for Democratic Affairs to President Nixon 1969-73. Convicted in 1974 (Watergate)

He has a knee-jerk response to everything.
Alastair Campbell, *The Daily Mirror*, of Anthony Beaumont-Dark

Governor Rockefeller has long since developed the knack of transforming expedience into an act of transcendent principle.
William F. Buckley Jr of Governor Nelson Rockefeller, *National Review*, 1963

ADVERTISING

I have nothing to do with any aspects of advertising; I can't even tell a Cinzano from a Martini. But I do trust the public to tell the difference between real life and advertisements, which is more than better educated worthies seem willing to do.
Edwina Currie MP, arguing in favour of BBC advertising and against the idea that advertising is bad for the public, 1989

ADVICE

Associate yourself with men of good quality if you esteem your own reputations; for 'tis better to be alone than in bad company.
George Washington (1732-99), *Rules of Civility*

Do what you can, with what you have, where you are.
Theodore Roosevelt (1858-1919)

In matters of principle, stand like a rock; in matters of taste, swim with the current.
Thomas Jefferson (1743-1826)

I have found the best way to give advice to your children is to find out what they want and then advise them to do it.
Harry S. Truman (1884-1972)

I heard the bullets whistle, and believe me there is something charming in the sound.
George Washington, *Presidential Anecdotes*

There is a homely adage which runs 'Speak softly and carry a big stick, you will go far'.
Theodore Roosevelt, 1901

Consider what you think justice requires, and decide accordingly. But never give your reasons; for your judgment will probably be right, but your reasons will certainly be wrong.
Earl of Mansfield (1705-93), British judge and politician, advising a new colonial governor

Never make people laugh. If you would succeed in life, you must be solemn, solemn as an ass. All the great monuments are built over solemn asses.
Thomas Corwin (1794-1865) American politician

No sex without responsibility.
Lord Longford, British social reformer, 1954

The first advice I am going to give my successor is to watch the generals and to avoid feeling that just because they were military men their opinions on military matters were worth a damn.
John F. Kennedy (1917-63)

Go West, young man, and grow up with the country.
Horace Greeley (1811-72) US politician and journalist, *Hints toward Reform*

The strongest possible piece of advice I would give to any young woman is: Don't screw around, and don't smoke.
Edwina Currie, 1988

Always remember others may hate you but those who hate you don't win unless you hate them. And then you destroy yourself.
Richard Nixon

Lighten up Al! Take a deep breath, inhale.
Dan Quayle during a television debate against Al Gore, Democratic Vice-presidential nominee, referring to Clinton's admission that he smoked pot at Oxford but didn't inhale

Don't quote Latin; say what you have to say, and then sit down.
Duke of Wellington (1769-1852), British General and statesman, advising a new MP

A G E

Being 70 is not a sin.
Golda Meir, 1971

I'd like to go on being 35 for a long time.
Margaret Thatcher, at age 54

I refuse to admit I'm more than 52 even if that
does make my sons illegitimate.
Nancy, Lady Astor (1879-1964)

It is fun to be in the same decade with you.
Franklin D. Roosevelt, after Churchill had
congratulated him on his 60th birthday

When they talk about his old age and
venerableness and nearness to the grave, he knows
better. He is like one of those cardinals, who as
quick as he is chosen Pope, throws away his
crutches and his crookedness, and is straight as a
boy. He is an old roué, who cannot live on slops,
but must have sulphuric acid in his tea.
Ralph Waldo Emerson, of John Q. Adams

Three things happen when you get to my age. First
your memory starts to go . . . and I have forgotten
the other two.
Denis Healey, aged 76

A L T E R N A T I V E S

I don't really know what they stand for. I saw
George Harrison and he wasn't sure what they
stood for either.
Ringo Starr, 1992, on the Natural Law Party

The reason they think I'm bonkers is because I
have original views and speak my mind.
Sir Nicholas Fairbairn, Conservative MP, 1993

In close-up the British revolutionary Left seethes
with such repulsive self-righteous dogmatists that
it practically drives one to enlist as a deck-hand on
Morning Cloud.
Richard Neville, 1972

The Loony Left have become so politically pure as to make Snow White look like a vamp.
Robert Kilroy-Silk, 1992

AMBITION

I would say Neil Kinnock, to get into Downing Street, would boil his granny for glue.
Jim Sillars, SNP 1992

Harold Wilson was the first Labour leader without a dream; his only dream was realised the day he became Labour leader.
Julie Burchill, author and journalist

ANALYSTS

I would not take too much notice of teenage scribblers in the City who jump up and down in an effort to get press attention.
Nigel Lawson, former Chancellor of the Exchequer, responding to City economists' predictions that interest rates would have to rise

The Chancellor's description of us as teenage scribblers is about as accurate as his forecast of the current account deficit – 100 per cent out.
Steve Bell, chief economist at Morgan Grenfell, 1988

APPEARANCE

Norman Fowler looks as if he is suffering from a famine and Nigel Lawson looks as though he caused it.
Neil Kinnock, Labour Party leader (1983-92)

Small, short-sighted, blonde, barbed – she reminds me of a bright little hedgehog.
Edwina Currie, of Teresa Gorman

I like the Tyrannosaurus Rex with his big teeth. It looks a bit like Michael Heseltine.
Neil Kinnock, 1992

It is an alarming thought that if we are ever invaded by monsters from outer space, the man who will be appointed to save us as Minister for Monsters will be this joke yobbo who could easily be mistaken for the traditional plumber with a cleft palate who has lost his dentures down the lavatory.
Auberon Waugh, *Private Eye,* of Denis Howell, Conservative MP

A fat slug.
Andrew Faulds, of Nigel Lawson

Nature has designed him along the lines of a professional mourner, a fourth form sneak or one of those woeful Victorian clerks who sat at their ledgers from dawn to dusk.
Jill Parkin, *The Daily Express,* 1992, of David Mellor

In Rochdale we've got Cyril Smith who's so fat he takes up most of the f***ing town.
Lisa Stansfield, singer, of her local MP

He was the Cabinet scruff, famous for his ghastly suede shoes, rumpled suits and hair that looked as if it had been cut by the council.
The Sunday Times, May 1993, of Kenneth Clarke

You'll never get on in politics, my dear, with that hair.
Nancy Astor, of Shirley Williams

Parkinson's red face looming over the dispatch-box is a pretty terrifying sight. I was not sure at one stage whether it was indignation, claret, or a faulty sun-lamp.
Peter Snape, of Cecil Parkinson

Maddox has the face of a three-month-old infant who is mean and bald and wears eye-glasses.
Norman Mailer, 1968, of Lestor Maddox

Cherie's floor-length skirt is very daring. Never in the history of British politics have we seen such a radical departure from the mid-calf norm.
Daily Mail on Cherie Blair, 1994

A R T S

Anyone who sees and paints a sky green and pastures blue ought to be sterilized.
Adolf Hitler (1889-1945)

Letting 100 flowers blossom and 100 schools of thought contend is the policy for promoting the progress of the arts and sciences.
Mao Tse-Tung (1893-1976), *Quotations from Chairman Mao*

A taste of sculpture and painting is – in my mind – as becoming as a taste of fiddling and piping is unbecoming to a man of fashion. The former is connected with history and poetry, the latter, with nothing that I know of but bad company.
Lord Chesterfield, 1749

I think it's the greatest monstrosity in America.
Harry S. Truman of the Old Executive Office Building, Washington, DC, 1958

If that's art, I'm a Hottentot!
Harry S. Truman

I can truthfully say that the painter has observed the Ten Commandments. Because he hath not made to himself the likeness of anything in heaven above, or that which is on earth beneath, or that which is in the water under the earth.
Abraham Lincoln

. . . Morse, your donkey is the saviour of your picture.
Abraham Lincoln, on a painting of Christ riding an ass into Jerusalem

It makes me look as if I was straining a stool.
Sir Winston Churchill, of his portrait by Graham Sutherland

He is a man whose contribution to the arts is about the same as Bluebeard's contribution to the institution of marriage.
Terry Dicks, of Tony Banks

Listening to him opining on the arts is rather like listening to Vlad the Impaler presenting *Blue Peter*.
Tony Banks, of Terry Dicks

If the Conservatives want to make the arts more popular and less nancy, well, I have my doubts about whether David Mellor is the one for the job.
Kenneth Branagh, actor and director, when Mellor was appointed as National Heritage Minister, 1992

The acronym of his remit Broadcasting, Arts, Sports, Television, Architecture, Recreation, Drama – adds up to BASTARD. So what does that make him?
The Sunday Telegraph, 1992

ASSASSINATION

They really are bad shots.
Charles de Gaulle, remark after narrowly escaping death in an assassination attempt

Please assure me that you are all Republicans!
Ronald Reagan, Republican President, addressing the surgeons on being wheeled into the operating theatre for an emergency operation after an assassination attempt

In Pierre Elliot Trudeau, Canada has at last produced a political leader worthy of assassination.
Irving Layton, Canadian poet

My family has learned a very cruel lesson of both history and fate.
Senator Edward Kennedy, on the assassination of his brother John Kennedy

I don't mind if my life goes in the service of the nation. If I die today every drop of my blood will invigorate the nation.
Indiri Gandhi (1917-84), Indian politician and Prime Minister. Remark the evening before she was assassinated

It is one of the incidents of the profession.
King Umberto 1 of Italy (1844-1900), after an attempt on his life

Tell my mother I died for my country. I thought I did for the best. Useless! Useless!
John Wilkes Booth (1838-1865), after his assassination of Abraham Lincoln

A desperate disease requires a dangerous remedy.
Guy Fawkes (1570-1606), Catholic conspirator on the gunpowder plot to blow up the Houses of Parliament

A X I O M S

It is a good thing to follow the First Law of Holes; if you are in one, stop digging.
Denis Healey, 1983

If you can't stand the heat, get out of the kitchen.
Harry S. Truman

If it walks like a duck, and quacks like a duck, then it just may be a duck.
Walter Reuther (1907-70) American trades union leader, on how to recognise a Communist

He who slings mud, usually loses ground.
Adlai Stevenson (1900-65), American politician and lawyer (attrib.)

B A N K I N G

I doubt if there is any occupation that is more consistently and unfairly demeaned, degraded, denounced and deplored than banking.
Senator William Proxmire, 1983

Banking establishments are more dangerous than standing armies.
Thomas Jefferson

BANKRUPTCY

Marvellous woman, by the way – not to bail me out. Like me she believes in private enterprise.
Sir Freddie Laker, founder of Laker Airways Ltd, referring to Mrs Thatcher following his company's collapse in 1982

BLOODY-MINDEDNESS

If the word 'No' was removed from the English language, he would be speechless.
John Hume, 1992, of Rev. Ian Paisley

He appears in the tradition of Hereward the Wake, fighting on against the Normans though all can see the cause is hopeless.
Lord Wyatt, of Arthur Scargill, President of the N.U.M.

The blunt-spoken New Englander ran the White House as the 'abominable no man'.
James Brooks, of Sherman Adams

His whole, huge carcass seemed to be made of iron. There was no give in him, no bounce, no softness. He sailed through American history like a steel ship loaded with monoliths of granite.
Henry L. Mencken, American Mercury, 1993, of Grover Cleveland

John Foster Dulles was a strong personality with views as narrow as a small-gauge railway.
Kim Philby (1911-88), British double agent

He is meticulously liberal – never ever has he erred in the direction of common sense, when the alternative was vote Liberal.
William F. Buckley Jr, of Eugene McCarthy, *On the Right,* 1967

BOOKS

When I want to read a book, I write one.
Benjamin Disraeli (1804-81), British statesman and novelist

Writing a book is an adventure: it becomes a mistress, then a master, and finally a tyrant.
Sir Winston Churchill

Life isn't all beer and skittles.
Thomas Hughes (1822-96), British novelist and Liberal MP, author of *Tom Brown's Schooldays*

It's more than a game. It's an institution.
Thomas Hughes, Tom Brown's Schooldays

To read too many books is harmful.
Mao Tse-Tung, 1977

Good, I've been using them quite a bit.
Ronald Reagan on receiving a present of an 1882 edition of *Russian Proverbs* from Mikhail Gorbachev

BRITAIN AND THE BRITISH

What is our task? To make Britain a fit country for heroes to live in.
David Lloyd George (1863-1945), Liberal statesman, 1918

We may be a small island, but we are not a small people.
Edward Heath, 1970

The charm of Britain has always been the ease with which one can move into the middle class.
Margaret Thatcher, 1974

The British disease is considering others more responsible than ourselves.
Geoffrey Howe, Chancellor of the Exchequer, *International Management,* 1986

Give the Germans five deutschmarks and they will save it. But give the British five pounds and they will borrow 25 pounds and spend it.
John Major, Chancellor of the Exchequer, 1990

Britain is not a country that is easily rocked by revolution . . . In Britain our institutions evolve. We are a Fabian society writ large.
Willie Hamilton MP, *My Queen and I*

I wish I could bring Stonehenge to Nyasaland to show there was a time when Britain had a savage culture.
Hastings Banda, Malawi statesman, 1963

If the British public falls for this, I say it will be stark, staring bonkers.
Baron Hailsham, Conservative politician, referring to Labour policy in the 1964 general-election campaign

Perhaps this country needs an iron lady.
Margaret Thatcher

BUREAUCRACY

The Treasury could not, with any marked success, run a fish and chip shop.
Harold Wilson, former Labour Prime Minister, 1984

The British Civil Service is a beautifully designed and effective braking system.
Shirley Williams, 1980

Britain has invented a new missile. It's called the civil service – it doesn't work and it can't be fired.
Sir Walter Walker, 1981

BUSINESS

The business of America is business.
Calvin Coolidge (1872-1933), US President, 1925

When you are skinning your customers, you should leave some skin on to grow so that you can skin them again.
Nikita Khrushchev (1894-1971) to British businessmen, 1961

The best executive is the one who has sense enough to pick good men to do what he wants done, and self restraint enough to keep from meddling with them while they do it.
Theodore Roosevelt

We demand that big business give people a square deal; in return we must insist that when anyone engaged in big business honestly endeavours to do right, he shall himself be given a square deal.
Theodore Roosevelt

Government in the USA today is a senior partner in every business in the country.
Norman Cousins, American editor and author

I studied the lives of great men and women, and I found that the men and women who got to the top were those who did the jobs they had in hand, with everything they had of energy and enthusiasm and hard work.
Harry S. Truman

We are running on Clinton time.
Clinton aides, admitting that he is frequently late for appointments

He'll be sitting there quietly reading a file and then he'll change the box over and there's a crash.
Norma Major, admitting she gets cross when her husband, John Major, does his boxes in bed, 1992

CAPITALISM

If you want to see the acceptable face of capitalism, go out to an oil rig in the North Sea.
Edward Heath 1974

We cannot remove the evils of capitalism without taking its source of power: ownership.
Neil Kinnock, British Labour politician, *Tribune,* 1975

Mr [Edward] Heath talked about the unacceptable face of capitalism, but intrinsically it doesn't have an unacceptable face.
Lord Weinstock, managing director, General Electric Co. plc., 1974

Capitalism is the exploitation of man by man. Communism is the complete opposite.
Polish proverb

Show me a capitalist and I'll show you a bloodsucker.
Malcolm X, American political and religious leader

Man is born perfect. It is the capitalist system which corrupts him.
Arthur Scargill, President, National Union of Mineworkers, 1981

When I was young, I worked for a capitalist 12 hours a day and I was always tired. Now I work for myself 20 hours a day and I never get tired.
Nikita Khrushchev

There is a serious tendency towards capitalism among the well-to-do peasants.
Mao Tse-Tung

Property is the fruit of labour; property is desirable; it is a positive good in the world. That some should be rich shows that others may become rich, and, hence, is just another encouragement to industry and enterprise.
Abraham Lincoln

Competition works. It is thanks to Freddie Laker that you can cross the Atlantic for so much less than it would have cost in the early 1970s.
Margaret Thatcher, speech, Conservative Party Conference, 1981

CHANCELLOR OF THE EXCHEQUER

The Chancellor of the Exchequer is a man whose duties make him more or less of a taxing machine. He is entrusted with a certain amount of misery which it is his duty to distribute as fairly as he can.
Viscount Robert Low (1811-92), British lawyer and politician, 1870

The most fabulous spender in history . . . skinning alive the middle classes.
Brendan Bracken, Chancellor 1945-47 on Hugh Dalton, 1946

Being Chancellor of the Exchequer is a humdrum activity.
Norman Lamont, Chancellor, 1990-93

This Budget gives away the money the Chancellor has not even borrowed yet.
Margaret Thatcher, then in opposition, referring to Denis Healey's 1976 Budget

I think it is the most back-breaking job in the government and indeed it has broken the back of nearly everyone who has held it since the war.
Roy Jenkins, Chancellor 1967-70, 1967

I think Edinburgh is a very flourishing city.
Margaret Thatcher, when asked if she considered Nigel
Lawson's budget to be brilliant, 1988

Quite the most brilliant we have seen, brilliant in
concept, brilliant in drafting and brilliant in
delivery.
Margaret Thatcher, replying when asked if she still
thought Nigel Lawson's budget was brilliant, 1988

He is to economic forecasting what Eddie The
Eagle is to ski-jumping.
Neil Kinnock on Nigel Lawson's 1989 budget

The successful conduct of economic policy is
possible only if there is – and is seen to be – full
agreement between the Prime Minister and the
Chancellor of the Exchequer . . . this essential
requirement cannot be satisfied as long as Alan
Walters remains your personal economic adviser.
Nigel Lawson in his resignation speech, 1989

When I heard the Prime Minister say what a
wonderful Chancellor she had, I knew he would
not last long.
Michael Foot MP, former leader, Labour Party, 1989

I am deeply uncomfortable being Chancellor with
this level of borrowing, I hate it.
Norman Lamont, interviewed by the *Guardian* on the
morning of his sacking, 1993

It'll cost you 10 pounds a question.
Mrs Irene Lamont [mother of Norman], who revealed
the Chancellor's resignation to the *Grimsby Evening
Telegraph,* 1993

May I congratulate the new Chancellor on the
rapid success of his policies?
Norman Lamont, on the announcement of a further fall
in unemployment seven weeks after he was fired

This is high passion politics. If you sack your
Chancellor, you know there will be a price to pay.
It always was that way, it always will be.
Michael Heseltine, referring to Norman Lamont's
dismissal

He suffers from what you may regard as a fatal
defect in a Chancellor. He is always wrong.
Iain MacLeod, of James Callaghan

Vatman!
Labour poster, 1992, of Chancellor Norman Lamont

I should have played something by Lamont-Dozier,
because there isn't anyone dozier than Lamont!
Peter Young, Jazz FM, Budget day, 1992

CHARACTER

. . . A great master of gibes and flouts and jeers.
Benjamin Disraeli, referring to Lord Salisbury, 1874

In defeat unbeatable; in victory unbearable.
Winston Churchill, of Field Marshal Montgomery of
Alamein

A nice man but someone who could be drawn into
a punch-up in a curry-house.
The Sun, 1992, of Neil Kinnock

John MacGregor is the Mad Hatter on the Titfield
Thunderbolt – unaware of his destination, time of
arrival, speed, safety or quality of his service.
John Prescott on the Transport Secretary's plans for
British Rail

You can tell a lot about a fellow's character from
the way he eats jelly beans.
Ronald Reagan

THE CITY

Seedy rather than fraudulent.
Roy Hattersley MP, on skulduggery in the City, 1986

You've got to twittle on for the City.
Geoffrey Howe MP, then Chancellor of the Exchequer,
explaining why Budget speeches take so long, 1982

CLANGERS

It will take some time, it always does, to change the economy. It's like turning the *Titanic* round, as you know.
John Major, then Chancellor of the Exchequer, 1990

COMMUNICATION

Political language – and with variations this is true of all political parties, from Conservatives to Anarchists – is designed to make lies sound truthful and murder respectable, and to give an appearance of solidity to pure wind.
George Orwell, Politics and the English Language, *Shooting an Elephant,* 1950

What I mean is that I'm fully seized of your aims and of course, I will do my utmost to see that they're put into practice. To that end, I recommend that we set up an interdepartmental committee with fairly broad terms of reference so that at the end of the day we'll be in a position to think through the various implications and arrive at a decision based on long-term considerations rather than rush prematurely into precipitate and possible ill-conceived action which might well have unforeseen repercussions.
Yes Minister, TV series purported to be a favourite of the Cabinet, 1980

You impress folks that little bit more with what you're saying if you say it nicely. People don't hear your ideas if you just stand there shouting out the words.
Lord Gormley, former president, National Union of Mineworkers, 1981

The Italians will laugh at me; every time Hitler occupies a country he sends me a message.
Benito Mussolini (1883-1945)

I used to tell my husband that, if he could make me understand something, it would be clear to all the other people in the country.
Eleanor Roosevelt, in her newspaper column, *My Day,* 1947

It is the President's decision to choose how to impart information to the people.
John Ehrlichman, assistant to Richard Nixon

I do not keep a diary. Never have. To write a diary every day is like returning to one's own vomit.
Enoch Powell, 1977

My father still reads the dictionary every day. He says your life depends on your power to master words.
Arthur Scargill, 1982

A memorandum is written not to inform the reader but to protect the writer.
Dean Acheson (attrib.)

At 3 o'clock
on Saturday afternoon
Theodore ROOSEVELT
WILL WALK
on the
WATERS OF LAKE MICHIGAN
Flyer distributed at Republican National Convention, 1912

It is sometimes said that face-to-face you don't see the other person's face.
Mikhail Gorbachev, after his second summit meeting with President Reagan, 1986

COMMUNISM

The government burns down whole cities while the people are forbidden to light lamps.
Mao Tse-Tung (attrib.)

Communism is Soviet power plus the electrification of the whole country.
Vladimir Ilyich Lenin (1870-1924), political slogan promoting the programme of electrification, 1920

The workers have nothing to lose but their chains. They have a world to gain. Workers of the World unite.
Karl Marx (1818-83), *The Communist Manifesto*

Every communist has a fascist frown, every fascist a communist smile.
Muriel Spark, British novelist, *The Girls of Slender Means*

Communism might be likened to a race in which all competitors come in first with no prizes.
Lord Inchcape, 1924

The illegitimate child of Karl Marx and Catherine the Great.
Clement Attlee, of Communism

History will, I believe, show that Communism was a phenomenon which, though it might have been born of idealism and a sense of injustice, in practice betrayed the very people it was alleged to serve.
The Queen, speaking in Hungary, 1993

Eisenhower told me never to trust a Communist.
Lyndon B. Johnson

He is a crypto-communist.
Margaret Thatcher, of Neil Kinnock

CONFESSIONS

Lord Tyrawley and I have been dead these two years, but we don't choose to have it known.
Lord Chesterfield (1694-1773), English statesman

CONGRESS

Congress – a body of men who meet to repeal laws.
Senate – a body of elderly gentlemen charged with high duties and misdemeanours.
Ambrose Bierce (1842-1914), American journalist

Congress would accomplish more with fewer 'blocs' and more tackle.
Columbia Record

Wonder if it would be possible to slow down a phonograph to where it could play 'The Congressional Record'.
Detroit News

Fleas can be taught nearly anything that a congressman can.
Mark Twain

Some statesmen go to Congress and some go to hell. It is the same thing, after all.
Eugene Field (1850-95), American writer

If the present Congress errs in too much talking, how can it be otherwise in a body to which the people send 150 lawyers.
Thomas Jefferson, in his autobiography

Office hours are twelve to one with an hour off for lunch.
George S. Kaufman (1889-1961), American playwright

The Senate is the last primitive society in the world. We still worship the elders of the tribe and honour the territorial imperative.
Eugene McCarthy

All I can say for the United States Senate is that it opens with prayer and closes with an investigation.
Will Rogers (1879-1935), humorist–philosopher

It could probably be shown by facts and figures that there is no distinctly native American criminal class except Congress.
Mark Twain

Reader, suppose you were an idiot; and suppose you were a member of Congress; but I repeat myself.
Mark Twain

CONSERVATIVE PARTY

A Conservative government is an organised hypocrisy.
Benjamin Disraeli, 1845

Their Europeanism is nothing but imperialism with an inferiority complex.
Denis Healey, referring to the policies of the Conservative Party, 1962

If capitalism depended on the intellectual quality of the Conservative Party, it would end about lunchtime tomorrow.
Tony Benn, Labour politician, 1989

The Tory Party, in so far as I am concerned are lower than vermin.
Aneurin Bevan

Conservatism offers no redress for the present, and makes no preparation for the future.
Benjamin Disraeli

A Conservative is a Liberal who got mugged the night before.
Frank Rizzo, 1972

A Conservative is a man who does not think anything should be done for the first time.
Frank Vanderlip

A Conservative is a man who thinks and sits; mostly sits.
Woodrow Wilson (1856-1924)

People are beginning to wish that the voters had been given breathometer tests when they voted in the present Conservative government.
William F. Buckley Jnr, On the Right, 1967

The Conservatives are nothing else but a load of kippers – two-faced and gutless.
Eric Heffer (1922-91), Labour politician

Kick the Tories out . . . and keep on kicking.
Socialist Worker, 1992

Fare-hiking, cost-cutting, congestion-creating, life-threatening, traffic-fuming, steam-powered.
John Prescott, on the Conservative transportation policy, 1992

It is as if Dickens' Mr Micawber is left hanging around with Beckett's Godot.
Neil Kinnock, on the Conservative's lack-lustre General Election campaign, 1992

C O V E R - U P S

Virtually every department of the Government is being sucked into the cover-up.
Jim Cousins MP, member of a Commons Select Committee inquiring into the Iraqi supergun affair, 1993

C O W A R D I C E

McKinley shows all the backbone of a chocolate éclair.
Theodore Roosevelt, of William McKinley

Unexceptional as a glass of decent Beaujolais.
Newsweek, 1965, of Adlai Stevenson

The real trouble with Stevenson is that he's no better than a regular sissy.
Harry S. Truman, of Adlai Stevenson

I don't relish the prospect of being skinned alive on Parliament Green if the Prime Minister was to win by one vote and I had abstained.
Andrew Faulds MP, Labour Europhile, on the Maastricht vote

You have chickened out. Run rabbit run rabbit, run, run, run.
Angry Labour MPs to Tory backbencher Michael Cartiss, a former Euro rebel explaining why he voted for the Government on Maastricht

CREDIT

I took a pair of old scissors. I cut the card into pieces and sent it back to them in their prepaid envelope with a letter protesting against a gross invasion of privacy.
Margaret Thatcher, on what she did upon receiving a credit card

I find it very useful to use a piece of plastic. But as far as I am concerned I always make a point to pay my credit card bill before coming into the period when you start paying interest.
Nigel Lawson MP, when Chancellor of the Exchequer, 1988

CRIME AND PUNISHMENT

Perhaps we should do something more drastic, like cutting their goolies off.
Teresa Gorman MP, on castration for rapists

If Toryism includes stealing from dukes, it is a Tory measure.
Enoch Powell MP, on leasehold reform plans, 1993

CRISIS

President Carter says that he doesn't panic in a crisis, but that's not the problem. The problem is that he panics without a crisis.
Clayton Fritchey

CRITICISM

Criticism may not be agreeable, but it is necessary. It fulfils the same function as pain in the body. It calls attention to an unhealthy state of things.
Sir Winston Churchill

I do not resent criticism, even when, for the sake of emphasis, it parts for the time with reality.
Sir Winston Churchill, 1941

He has a right to criticise, who has a heart to help.
Abraham Lincoln

Dread death alone could place embargo
Upon the tongue and pen of Margot.
Kensal Green, of Margot Asquith

He never wrote an invitation to dinner without an eye on posterity.
Benjamin Disraeli, of writer and politician, Edward Bulwer

He's a bitter and twisted little man.
Andrew Hunt MP, reacting to Lamont's Commons assault on John Major

The criticism that Norman Lamont made yesterday is frankly ludicrous.
Sir Norman Fowler, reacting to Lamont's Commons assault on John Major

CUBA

A revolution is not a bed of roses. A revolution is a struggle to the death between the future and the past.
Fidel Castro, Cuban statesman, on the second anniversary of the Revolution, 1961

The worse I do, the more popular I get.
John F. Kennedy, referring to his popularity following the 'Bay of Pigs'

I guess this is the week I earn my salary.
John F. Kennedy, during the Cuban missiles crisis, 1962

They talk about who won and who lost. Human reason won. Mankind won.
Nikita Khrushchev, referring to the Cuban missiles crisis

DECEIT

He is one of the most unfaithful deceivers, with a coating of intellectual cheap glitter.
Hugh Dalton, of Richard Crossman

Utterly unscrupulous. Moral principle was not his strong suit.
Lord Hailsham, of Richard Crossman

He was a heavyweight intellect with a lightweight judgment.
Denis Healey, of Richard Crossman

I'm as Welsh as nutty slack but I can see through Neil Kinnock's red mist of deceit easily. I know histrionics when I see them.
Ruth Madoc, actress, 1992

Nodding and winking and grinning, a foot-in-the-door salesman trying to sell you a gentle, harmless, semi-demi socialism.
John Major, 1992, of Neil Kinnock

The word honour in the mouth of Mr Webster is like the word love in the mouth of a whore.
Ralph Waldo Emerson, of Daniel Webster

DEMOCRACY

A democracy is a government in the hands of men of low birth, no property, and vulgar employments.
Aristotle (384-322 BC), Greek philosopher, *Politics,* *c.*322 BC

Democracy is a government by discussion, but it is only effective if you can stop people talking.
Clement Attlee, *Anatomy of Britain*

Democracy substitutes election by the incompetent many for appointment by the corrupt few.
George Bernard Shaw (1856-1950), Irish playwright, *Man and Superman*

Our great democracies still tend to think that a stupid man is more likely to be honest than a clever man, and our politicians take advantage of this prejudice by pretending to be even more stupid than nature made them.
Bertrand Russell, New Hope for a Changing World, 1951

Democracy means government by the uneducated, while aristocracy means government by the badly educated.
G. K. Chesterton (1874-1936)

The government of bullies, tempered by editors.
Ralph Waldo Emerson

The art of running the circus from the monkey cage.
Henry L. Mencken (1880-1956), American journalist and linguist

Democracy is the theory that the common people know what they want, and deserve to get it good and hard.
Henry L. Mencken

Democracy is hypocrisy without limitation.
Iskander Mirza, 1958

An institution in which the whole is equal to the scum of the parts.
Keith Preston (1884-1927), American poet

Proportional Representation, I think, is fundamentally counter-democratic.
Neil Kinnock, Marxism Today, 1983

Democracy is a form of religion. It is the worship of jackals by jackasses.
Henry L. Mencken (1880-1956)

DEMOCRATIC PARTY

I come from a state that raises corn and cotton
and cockleburs and Democrats, and frothy
eloquence neither convinces me nor satisfies me. I
am from Missouri. You have got to show me.
Willard L. Duncan Vandiver (1854-1932), American
politician, 1899

The Democratic Party is like a mule – without
pride of ancestry or hope of posterity.
Edmund Burke

I never said all democrats were saloon-keepers;
what I said was all saloon-keepers were
Democrats.
Horace Greeley (1811-72)

They have made inflated claims about what they
intend to do. But that's only to be expected, since
they are the party of inflation.
Ronald Reagan, 1988

The leaders of the Democratic Party have gone so
far left, they've left the country.
Ronald Reagan

I belong to no organised party – I am a Democrat.
Will Rogers

DETERMINATION

The trouble with Winston is that he nails his
trousers to the mast and can't climb down.
Clement Attlee, of Sir Winston Churchill

DICTATORS

Fascism is not an article for export.
Benito Mussolini, 1932

The essential thing is the formation of the political
will of the nation: that is the starting point for
political action.
Adolf Hitler, 1932

You do your worst, and we will do our best.
Sir Winston Churchill in a speech addressed to Hitler,
1941

I often think how much easier the world would
have been to manage if Herr Hitler and Signor
Mussolini had been at Oxford.
Viscount Halifax (1881-1959), British politician, 1937

The crafty, cold-blooded, black-hearted Italian.
Sir Winston Churchill, British statesman, referring to
Benito Mussolini, 1941

In politics, as in grammar, one should be able to
tell the substantives from the adjectives. Mussolini
was only an adjective. Hitler was a nuisance.
Mussolini was bloody. Together a bloody nuisance.
Salvador de Madariaga y Rogo (1886-1978), Spanish
diplomat and writer (attrib.)

The destiny of history has united you with myself
and the Duce in an indissoluble way.
General Franco (1892-1975), Dictator of Spain, 1939-
75, in a letter to Adolf Hitler

DRINK

It would be better that England should be free
than that England should be compulsorily sober.
William Connor Magee (1821-91), British clergyman,
on the Intoxicating Liquor Bill, 1928

DUTY

The duty of an opposition is to oppose.
Lord Randolph Churchill (1849-95), British
Conservative politician, 1872

Compassion is not a sloppy, sentimental feeling for people who are underprivileged or sick . . . it is an absolutely practical belief that, regardless of a person's background, ability or inability to pay, he should be provided with the best that society has to offer.
Neil Kinnock, in his Maiden Speech, House of Commons, 1970

A politician is someone who lies down for his party.
Paddy Ashdown

ECONOMICS

You cannot feed the hungry on statistics.
David Lloyd George, advocating Tariff reform, 1904

A fully equipped Duke costs as much to keep up as two Dreadnoughts, and Dukes are just as great a terror, and they last longer.
David Lloyd George, 1909

They can no more pontificate on economics than the Pope could correct Galileo on physics.
John Selwyn Gummer MP, on the Church's right to intervene in the economic debate, 1984

You know what you can do best, and you know what is best that you do.
Margaret Thatcher, to Prof. Alan Walters, when she appointed him as her economic adviser, 1989

Who can resist a date with a blonde? She always wanted me to come back. By God I've been lucky, haven't I?
Prof. Alan Walters, on his reappointment as economic adviser to Margaret Thatcher, 1988

He is Mr Rising Price himself.
Iain MacLeod, on Hugh Gaitskell (1906-63), Labour MP

THE ECONOMY

Indeed, let's be frank about it; some of our people have never had it so good.
Harold Macmillan, 1957

. . . trying to ride a bicycle on a cliff path – if you get it wrong one way, you bruise your elbow which is disagreeable. If you get it wrong the other way you fall 1,000 feet.
Roy Jenkins, on running the economy, 1981

Recession is when the woman next door loses her job. Slump is when the woman in your house loses her job. Recovery is when the woman in No. 10 loses hers.
Len Murray, former General Secretary Trades Union Congress, 1983

We've got a loadsamoney economy – and behind it comes loadsatrouble.
Neil Kinnock, 1988

The way to stop financial joy-riding is to arrest the chauffeur, not the automobile.
Woodrow Wilson

Everybody is in favour of general economy and particular expenditure.
Anthony Eden (1897-1977), former Prime Minister, 1956

When I have to read economic documents I have to have a box of matches and start moving them into position to illustrate and simplify the points to myself.
Sir Alec Douglas-Home, former Prime Minister

You cannot go to sleep with one form of economic system and wake up the next morning with another.
Mikhail Gorbachev, 1990

It would be very superficial to think that the Soviet Union can be bought for dollars.
Mikhail Gorbachev, 1990

We now have the Frank Sinatra doctrine. He has a song: *I did it my way.* So every country decides on its own which road to take.
Gennady Gerasimov, then Soviet Foreign Ministry spokesman, on whether other Eastern bloc countries should follow the Russian path of reform, 1989

In other words, in moving towards the market we are moving not away from socialism, but towards a fuller realisation of society's capabilities.
Mikhail Gorbachev, 1990

She's a handbag economist who believes that you pay as you go.
New Yorker, of Margaret Thatcher, 1986

Starring John Major, the Conservatives' very own box-office disaster – *Honey I Shrank the Economy.*
John Smith (1938-94), Labour leader

I always knew that Neil Kinnock belonged in the economic nursery. Now, God help us, we've got twins.
Michael Heseltine, 1992, of John Smith, then Deputy Leader of the Labour Party

He has as much likelihood of understanding how the economy works as Donald Duck has of winning Mastermind.
John Major, of John Smith

EDUCATION AND TRAINING

For all too many years people went to schools which despised the world of work and went to universities which totally rejected it.
Lord Young of Graffham, former Secretary of State for Trade and Industry, 1985

God help those who train themselves.
Lord Young of Graffham, 1983

We propose to streamline the tests.
John Patten, backing down on National Curriculum tests for 14-year-olds, 1993

Whenever the cause of the people is entrusted to professors it is lost.
Nikolai Lenin

Thank you very much for that warm welcome.
John Patten, Education Secretary, after being hissed and booed by headmasters, 1993

A man who has never gone to school may steal from a freight car; but if he has a university education, he may steal the whole railroad.
Theodore Roosevelt

A child miseducated is a child lost.
John F. Kennedy

Why should we subsidise intellectual curiosity?
Ronald Reagan

When I was a young man in the House, I decided that the best qualification for a politician was to enjoy Dostoevsky.
Denis Healey MP, 1993

He didn't really stand out. He wasn't particularly bright. I'd say he was average, but a nice lad. Of course his name was pronounced differently then.
Teacher at Lerwick Primary School, of the young Norman Lamont, 1993

You've been strutting around the dispatch box like a puffed-up peacock on heat. Today you've come in like a bedraggled battery hen that's laid its last egg.
Dennis Skinner, Labour MP, of John Patten, Education Secretary's plan to review tests for 14-year-olds

Having been a London teacher with nubile young girls in my care, I know quite well that it is not always possible to restrain their behaviour. Rather than ending up at the age of fourteen with babies to look after there is something to be said for some form of counselling. If we can't do that, we should protect them.
Teresa Gorman MP, backing the Health Minister's recommendation to supply condom machines in schools, 1993

Just because you swallowed a fucking dictionary when you were about 15 doesn't give you the right to pour a bucket of shit over the rest of us.
Paul Keating, Australian finance minister, responding to a critic of his schooling, 1989

E G O

He is incapable of working in a team. He's like an Upas tree which poisons the ground for miles around.
Denis Healey

He is distrustful, obstinate, excessively vain, and takes no counsel from anyone.
Thomas Jefferson, of Dean Acheson

It has been a political career of this man to begin with hypocrisy, proceed with arrogance, and to finish with contempt.
Tom Paine, of Dean Acheson

I have a touch of regret that I didn't become Prime Minister.
Lord Norman Tebbit MP, 1993

My strength has always been on the street.
Lord Jeffrey Archer MP and novelist

ELECTIONS

I will not accept if nominated and will not serve if elected.
General William Sherman (1820-91), US politician and president, replying to a request that he accept the Republican presidential nomination (attrib.)

Be Thankful Only One of Them Can Win.
Bumper sticker, Nixon/Kennedy presidential election, 1960

If Voting Changed Anything, They'd Make It Illegal.
Badge, London 1983

People on whom I do not bother to dote
Are people who do not bother to vote.
Ogden Nash, Election Day is a Holiday, *Happy Days,* 1933

Vote for the man who promises least; he'll be the least disappointing.
Bernard M. Baruch, American businessman and presidential adviser

I have decided to vote Labour. I don't like Kinnock, but I think he's a bad front to quite a lot of good men, while John Major is a good front to quite a lot of bad men.
Katherine Hamnett, British fashion designer, at the build-up of the 1992 elections

Personally, I'm not much of a betting man and it's so far away. I wouldn't invest money myself at this stage.
John Major, on bookmakers' election odds

It's as lively as necrophilia.
Austin Mitchell, on the election campaign, 1992

I used to tell people to ski down butter mountains but that didn't win any votes.
Stuart Hughes, Raving Loony Green Giant Party

You can't make a soufflé rise twice.
Alice Roosevelt-Longworth, 1948, on his second presidential nomination

His [presidential] campaign kickoff was so dismal that it needed a plastic surgeon instead of a press agent to put a face on it.
Jane Mayer, of Walter Mondale, *Wall Street Journal,* 1984

EQUALITY

I have a dream that one day this nation will rise up, live out the true meaning of its creed: we hold these truths to be self-evident, that all men are created equal.
Martin Luther King (1929-68), US clergyman and civil rights leader, 1963

Having a baby boy is where feminist theory collides into reality with a juddering crash.
Diane Abbott, Labour MP and mother of a 20-month-old son, 1993

Equality of opportunity means equal opportunity to be unequal.
Iain Macleod (1913-70), British politician

All men are born equal, but quite a few eventually get over it.
Lord Mancroft, 1967

Once a woman is made man's equal, she becomes his superior.
Margaret Thatcher

I want to be the white man's brother, not his brother-in-law.
Martin Luther King, 1962

I don't consider the Equal Rights Amendment a political issue. It is a moral issue as far as I am concerned. Where are women mentioned in the Constitution except in the Nineteenth Amendment, giving us the right to vote? When they said all men were created equal, they really meant it – otherwise, why did we have to fight for the Nineteenth Amendment?
Carol Burnett, US comedienne and actress, *San Francisco Chronicle,* 1979

Well, it's hard for a mere man to believe that woman doesn't have equal rights.
Dwight D. Eisenhower

ESTATE AGENTS

She took the country off the landowners and gave it to the estate agents.
Denis Healey MP, on Margaret Thatcher, 1987

Whenever I am told that politicians are among the lowest forms of life, I thank God I am not an estate agent.
Jack Straw MP, 1989

ETHICS

We had no use for the policy of the Gospels; if someone slaps you, just turn the other cheek. We had shown that anyone who slapped us on our cheek would get his head kicked off.
Nikita Khrushchev (1894-1971), Soviet statesman, *Khrushchev Remembers*

If I weren't so fond of her I'd call them the Mary Whitehouse of the investment world.
Norman Tebbit MP, on ethical investors, 1990

As far as I am concerned, dirty tricks are part and parcel of effective government.
Alan Clark, former Defence Minister, 1993

What has Britain come to and where is there left any integrity in Cabinet ministers and officers of the Crown?
Simon Hughes, Liberal Democrat MP on the Lamont affair, 1993

You can't adopt politics as a profession and remain honest.
Louis McHenry Howe (1871-1936), US diplomat, 1933

There will be no whitewash in the White House.
Richard Nixon referring to the Watergate scandal, 1973

I am not a crook.
Richard Nixon (attrib.)

President Nixon's motto was, if two wrongs don't make a right, try three.
Norman Cousins, 1979

The whole saga has unfolded like a Greek tragedy. And 18 months later I have lost the job I loved.
Michael Mates, on his involvement in the Asil Nadir affair, 1993

We are faced with a choice between the work ethic that built this nation's character – and the new welfare ethic that could cause the American character to weaken.
Richard Nixon

If you start throwing hedgehogs under me, I shall throw two porcupines under you.
Nikita Khrushchev, 1963

Victorian values . . . were the values when our country became great.
Margaret Thatcher, 1982

Without doubt the greatest injury . . . was done by basing morals on myth, for sooner or later myth is recognised for what it is, and disappears. The morality loses the foundation on which it has been built.
Herbert Samuel (1870-1963), statesman and philosophical writer, 1947

He had an undigested system of ethics.
John Q. Adams, of Henry Clay

E U R O P E   A N D   T H E   E C

In Western Europe there are now only small countries – those that know it and those that don't know it yet.
Theo Lefevre (1914-73), Belgian Prime Minister, 1961-65

It would not be in Britain's, or, I believe, Europe's interest to join the present half-baked system.
Prof. Alan Walters, referring to the European Monetary System, 1989

This is all a German racket designed to take over the whole of Europe. It has to be thwarted. This rushed takeover by the Germans on the worst possible basis, with the French behaving like poodles to the Germans, is absolutely intolerable.
Nicholas Ridley MP, then Trade and Industry Secretary, on European monetary union, shortly before resigning from the Government, 1990

There are those who want an economic and monetary union so beautiful, so perfect, that it will never get started, it will never even be born.
Jacques Delors, president, EC Commission, 1990

Now you [the British] want to come in, and you not only want to come in, but you want a special deal. And furthermore, if you come in, others will come in with you out of the European Free Trade Agreement group. And even with the best will in the world on your part and no matter what promises you make, you are just going to change things in our little club. And the changes are going to be profoundly disturbing and upsetting, and I just don't like it. This is nothing against you personally or against your country. You know the way I feel about you. It is just simply that something comfortable that works is going to be changed and I would prefer not to have it changed.
Charles de Gaulle (1890-1970), former French President, to Harold Macmillan, on Britain's desire to join the Common Market

I do not see the EC as a great love affair. It is more like nine middle-aged couples with failing marriages meeting at a Brussels hotel for a group grope.
Kenneth Tynan (1927-80), 1975

European Community institutions have produced European beets, butter, cheese, wine, veal and even pigs. But they have not produced Europeans.
Louise Weiss MEP, 1980

It is the people's turn to speak. It is their powers of which we are the custodians.
Margaret Thatcher, calling for a referendum on Maastricht, 1993

The best thing about Britain is that it is not Holland, which is so flat, and the people are nuts, and it's where Maastricht lives.
Alice Thomas Ellis, writer, 1993

The Spanish delegation is in no hurry. When I say in no hurry at all at this time of day, I mean in no hurry.
Miguel Gil, Spanish spokesman, at an early-evening briefing

We have to end the uncertainty on the Maastricht treaty which I think is one of the causes of the economic situation.
Jacques Poos, Luxembourg Foreign Minister, Edinburgh Summit, 1992

I was ready mentally and physically to go until tomorrow.
François Mitterand, Edinburgh Summit, 1992

I made a considerable verbal contribution.
Helmut Kohl, German Chancellor, on how he prevented Spain from blocking a deal, Edinburgh Summit, 1992

You have those who are paying and those who are receiving. So everybody who's receiving wants to get as much as they can and everybody who's paying wants to pay as little as they can.
Albert Reynolds, Irish Prime Minister, Edinburgh Summit, 1992

This is not for discussion. Otherwise I walk out and you can forget about your package.
Helmut Kohl, when some tried to reopen discussion of extra parliament seats for Germany, Edinburgh Summit, 1992

The matter of the timing of the Maastricht treaty is a matter for the British parliament, is now and will remain a matter for the British parliament and for no one else.
John Major, Edinburgh Summit, 1992

All I want to say, particularly to our partners . . . is don't push it, don't push it, because that isn't going to help us get it through.
Norman Lamont, Chancellor of the Exchequer, of the Maastricht treaty

Maastricht is like that famous dead parrot. They may try to nail it on the perch again but nobody will believe it is still alive.
Norman Tebbit MP

I am often asked if non-political people talk to me about Maastricht. The answer is yes – the most common question is: When will this bloody Maastricht thing finish?
George Robertson, Labour Foreign Affairs spokesman

They [the Government] seem to be treating Maastricht like a rubber duck; shape it, twist it, bite it, alter it, it springs back into shape.
Jack Cunningham, Labour Foreign Affairs spokesman.

That foul abomination, that running sore of Britain's politics, John Major's political tar baby, John Smith's self-imposed political ball and chain, the crumbling altar of the xenophobic paranoiac world of Monsieur Delors.
Norman Tebbit on the Maastricht Treaty

They tried to demoralise me, but as far as I am concerned they were just abusing me.
Teresa Gorman MP, on the Whips pressure to vote for Maastricht

I am having difficulty knowing what today's debate is about.
Geoffrey Dickens, on the Maastricht debate

We will remain Germans, Britons, Italians and Frenchmen.
Helmut Kohl

It is absurd for us to be blamed for being right. It has been a case of the incredible in pursuit of the impossible.
Bill Cash, leader of the Tory Euro rebels, on the collapse of the ERM

Not tonight Josephine. We'll debate it at some other time.
John Major to Labour leader John Smith, on the Maastricht debate

This is becoming more fun than I had imagined.
John Major, during the Maastricht debate

This is the last speech, in the last debate, on the Maastricht treaty.
Douglas Hurd (to cheers)

Nothing was asked for, nothing was offered and nothing was given.
John Major, denying deals with Ulster unionists

The Prime Minister has got the Parliamentary Party by the goolies.
Teresa Gorman, Euro sceptic

This government hasn't even got whips and tellers who are capable of counting. No wonder this country is up to its neck in debt.
Dennis Skinner, Labour MP

After the Maastricht negotiations, you said it was game, set and match for the UK. Nineteen months later, after endless foot faults, double faults and mis-hits, you were struggling with a tie break. And now like some petulant tennis prima donna, you are threatening to take your racket away.
Parliament must put the stalemate over Maastricht behind it. The boil must be lanced.
John Smith, Labour leader, attacking John Major, before the Maastricht vote

It is the people's turn to speak. It is their powers of which we are custodians.
Margaret Thatcher, calling for a referendum on Maastricht

The survival of the Conservative Government is not at stake. What is at stake is the survival of a credible European policy.
Douglas Hurd, Foreign Secretary, after the Maastricht Treaty was passed

I am not impressed by being called anti-European by those who were in short trousers when I began campaigning for Britain to enter the Common Market.
Norman Tebbit, 1993

I saw him [Norman Tebbit] in the members lobby trying to persuade new members to vote against the Government.
Edward Heath, 1993

EVASION

His successive attempts to find a policy remind me of a chorus of a third-rate review. His evasions reappear in different scenes and in new dresses, and every time they dance with renewed and despairing vigour. But it is the same old jig.
Lord Beaverbrook, of Stanley Baldwin

Michael Heseltine is to accuracy what Gary Glitter is to good taste.
Bryan Gould, 1992

FAME

Aye, I remember the Lam'nt lad. He's an arrogant little bugger, you know. I don't think he's fit for the job he's doing at all. I was in the bank for 49 years and nine months. After he had been working in a bank for a year he thought he knew more than I did.
Harry Drever, former manager of the Bank of Scotland, Lerwick, of Chancellor Norman Lamont, 1993

I should like to be known as a former President who minded his own business.
Calvin Coolidge

I shall never get used to not being the most beautiful woman in the room. It was an intoxication to sweep in and know every man had turned his head. It kept me in form.
Lady Randolph Churchill (Jennie)

FAMILY

I murdered my grandmother this morning.
Franklin D. Roosevelt, his habitual greeting to any guest at the White House he suspected of paying no attention to what he said

An extremely protective, secretive, old-style WASP who has been able to project herself as an earth mother with no real proof.
Andrew Sullivan, New Republic, of Barbara Bush, wife of George

The former 'First Brat' has become a Yippie of yuppiedom.
Don Lesse, of Amy Carter, daughter of Jimmy Carter, Boston Globe, 1987

Jimmy Carter needs Billy like Van Gogh needs stereo.
Johnny Carson, of Billy Carter, brother of Jimmy, 1977

The one thing I do not want to be called is the First Lady. It sounds like a saddle horse.
Jackie Kennedy, wife of John F. Kennedy

I didn't much like it when Mr Nixon and his wife started matching me up with their eldest daughter. Which one is she, Tricia, isn't that right? I found her artificial and plastic.
Prince Charles, of Tricia Nixon, daughter of Pat and Richard

The First Toothpick.
Julie Burchill, of Nancy Reagan, wife of Ronald

He is used to dealing with estate workers. I cannot see how anyone can say he is out of touch.
Lady Caroline Douglas-Home, daughter of Alec, referring to her father's suitability for his new role as Prime Minister, 1963

I do, and I also wash and iron them.
Denis Thatcher, British businessman and husband of Margaret, when asked 'Who wears the pants in this house?'

You can get used to anything if you have to, even to feeling perpetually guilty.
Golda Meir, on her inattention to her children

Sometimes when I look at my children I say to myself, 'Lillian, you should have stayed a virgin'.
Lillian Carter

The kind of man who thinks that helping with the dishes is beneath him will also think that helping with the baby is beneath him, and then he certainly is not going to be a very successful father.
Eleanor Roosevelt

It's shattering to be told your father stinks.
Julie Nixon, daughter of Richard

Nobody could sleep with Dick. He wakes up during the night, switches on the lights, speaks into his tape recorder, or takes notes – it's impossible.
Pat Nixon, wife of Richard

It takes two to make a marriage a success and only one a failure.
Herbert Samuel (1870-1963), British Liberal statesman and philosopher

A Cabinet Minister's wife needs a good hobby. I don't think there is much for a Cabinet Minister's wife to do in London.
What should decide Ken's reputation is how he does his job, not anything else. I prefer to keep in the background.
Gillian Clarke, wife of Kenneth, shortly after he took up his new role as Chancellor of the Exchequer, 1993

I think if Barbara Bush were running this year
she'd be elected, but it's too late.
George Bush, when elected as president, speaking of his
wife's popularity

I am Hillary, hear me roar
I'm more important than Alan Gore
I could run this country if I had the chance
Got an office down the hall
Now Bill can't fool around at all
In this White House I wear the pants
Oh, yes, I'm his wife, but I'm in love with politics
Yes this is my life, I might run in '96.
I am Hillary, a song which topped the charts of a
Washington radio station, 1993

I can't remember so many stories about a First
Lady.
Ben Bradlee, a friend of President Kennedy and editor of
the *Washington Post* when it broke the Watergate story,
admitting the popularity of Hillary Clinton

Q: Why has the Secret Service tripled its protection
staff for Hillary Clinton?
A: Because if she gets killed, Bill Clinton will
become president.

Q: Why doesn't Hillary wear mini-skirts?
A. Because she doesn't want to show she is the
man of the family.

No, I'm too tired, I would rather just go home and
sleep.
Peter Lilley, Social Security Secretary, when asked by his
wife if he would like to go to Paris for the weekend to
celebrate the sale of all of her paintings at a two-day
exhibition at the London Mall Gallery, 1992

Alan is telling me to be more French. He is
terrifically difficult half the time, and makes you
want to throttle him. But you still love him.
Jane Clark, wife of former Defence Minister, Alan, on
her husband's reputation as a womaniser

We have become a grandmother.
Margaret Thatcher, on the birth of her first grandchild,
1989

The vast majority of single mothers do not choose
to be single parents. But if they do, I personally
don't agree with them.
Tony Blair, Leader of the Labour Party, 1994

F A S C I S M

Fascism is a religion; the twentieth century will be
known in history as the century of Fascism.
Benito Mussolini, on Hitler's seizing power

Fascism is not an article for export.
Benito Mussolini, 1932

F A U X   P A S

Cor, you look just like the Prime Minister. You
ought to get a job as one of those lookalikes.
Comment from a couple of technicians to Terry Major-Ball,
the Prime Minister's brother, 1993

This is a rotten argument, but it should be good
enough for their lordships on a hot summer
afternoon.
Anon. Note on a ministerial brief read out by mistake in
the House of Lords

Chappaquidick: the name of a place brought up by
candidates every time they say they are not going
to bring it up.
Mark Russell, Presenting Mark Russell, referring to
Edward Kennedy, 1980

I always get my fives and threes muddled up.
Norman Lamont, Chancellor of the Exchequer, getting
his figures in a tangle trying to explain why Britain needed
to borrow £50 billion, 1993

Well, nobody is dead. At the end of this opera
everybody's dead.
Sir Patrick Mayhew, after being told nearly 30 people
had been injured in a Belfast explosion, while at the opera
to see *Lucia di Lammermoor*

FEMINISM

The male is by nature superior and the female inferior; one rules and the other is ruled.
Aristotle (384-322 BC), Greek philosopher, *Politics,* Book 1, 4th century BC

What a Woman may be, and yet not have the Vote:
Mayor Nurse Mother Doctor or Teacher Factory Hand
What a Man may have been and yet not lose the Vote:
Convict Lunatic Proprietor of White Slaves Unfit for Service Drunkard
Poster used during the Suffragette campaign, 1901

We want the electoral franchise not because we are angels oppressed by the wickedness of the 'base wretch of man' but because we want women to have the ennobling influence of national responsibility brought into their lives.
Millicent Garrett Fawcett (1847-1929), British suffragette

Many Lancashire women are keeping on homes, and even worthless husbands, and yet the latter when it becomes a matter of voting have the only voice in the affairs of the nation. The children are led by this to think little of their mothers and much of their fathers.
Sarah Dickenson (1868-1954), British suffragette, 1901

Give women the vote, and in five years there will be a crushing vote on bachelors.
George Bernard Shaw (1856-1950), Irish dramatist and critic, *Man and Superman*

Just so long as there is a degraded class of labour in the market, it always will be used by the capitalists to checkmate and undermine the superior classes.
Susan B. Anthony (1820-1906), US editor, 1906

If all women were enfranchised they would at once swamp the votes of men.
Samuel Evans MP for Glamorgan, Wales, House of Commons, 1906

I see some rats have got in; let them squeal, it doesn't matter.
David Lloyd George (1863-1945), British Liberal statesman, when suffragettes interrupted a meeting, 1908

The story of women's work in gainful employments is a story of constant changes or shiftings of work and workshop, accompanied by long hours, low wages, insanitary conditions, overwork, and the want on the part of the woman of training, skill, and vital interest in her work.
Helen L. Sumner (1876-1933), US government official and children's rights activist, Senate Report, 1911

People are led to reason thus: a woman who is a wife is one who has made a permanent sex bargain for her maintenance; the woman who is not married must therefore make a temporary bargain of the same kind.
Christabel Pankhurst (1880-1958), British suffragette, 1913

Political equality is Dead Sea fruit unless it leads to economic equality.
Vera Brittain (1893-1970), British writer and feminist, 1931

Women get more unhappy the more they try to liberate themselves and act like men. A woman is a tender and sweet person and she'll lose that if she tries to be like a man.
Brigitte Bardot, French film actress, 1973

She will be challenging a system that is still wedded to militarism and that saves billions of dollars a year by underpaying women and using them as a reserve cheap labour supply.
Bella Abzug, US lawyer and congresswoman, referring to a woman politician, 1974

There are very few jobs that actually require a penis or vagina. All other jobs should be open to everybody.
Florynce R. Kennedy, US lawyer and civil rights activist

Anybody against women, against the era, should never be voted into office again.
Liz Carpenter, US writer and feminist, 1979

Nobody wants me as a Cabinet Minister and they are perfectly right. I am an agitator, not an administrator.
Nancy Astor

I stopped believing in Santa Claus at an early age. Mother took me to see him in a department store and he asked me for my autograph.
Shirley Temple Black, US politician and former child film star

To be a liberated woman is to renounce the desire of being a sex object or a baby girl. It is to acknowledge that the Cinderella-Prince Charming story is a child's fairy tale.
Clare Booth Luce, US politician and writer, 1974

Feminism is an entire world view of *gestalt,* not just a laundry list of 'women's issues'.
Charlotte Bunch, US editor, feminist, educator and writer, *New Directions for Women,* 1981

FOREIGN EXCHANGE

All the little gnomes of Zurich and other finance centres.
Harold Wilson, on international speculators, 1956

I don't give a shit about the lira.
Richard Nixon, on the deteriorating Italian currency, revealed in the Watergate tapes

From now on the pound is worth 14 per cent or so less in terms of other currencies. It does not mean, of course, that the pound here in Britain, in your pocket or purse or in your bank has been devalued.
Harold Wilson, on the devaluation of the pound, 1967

I hope no one is going to bring sterling into this election. Sterling should always be above politics.
Harold Wilson, then Labour leader, 1966

FOREIGN POLICY

The American continents, by the free and independent condition which they have assumed and maintain, are henceforth not to be considered as subject for future colonisation by any European powers . . . In the wars of the European powers in matters relating to themselves we have never taken any part, nor does it comport with our policy to do so.
James Monroe (1758-1831), US President, making a statement of principle that, as the 'Monroe Doctrine', became a cornerstone of US foreign policy, 1823

He saw foreign policy through the wrong end of a municipal drainpipe.
David Lloyd George, referring to Neville Chamberlain

He has crawled so far up the backside of N.A.T.O. that you can't see the soles of his feet.
Ken Livingstone, of Gerald Kaufman

I wouldn't say she was open-minded on the Middle-East so much as empty-headed. She probably thinks that Sinai is the plural of sinus.
Jonathan Aitken, of Margaret Thatcher

The power of positive brinking.
Adlai Stevenson, on John Foster Dulles' foreign policies

When Kissinger can get the Nobel Peace Prize, what is there left for satire?
Tom Lehrer, of President Henry Kissinger

Well, I learned a lot. You'd be surprised. They're all individual countries.
Ronald Reagan, following a tour of South America, 1982

FREEDOM

Those who deny freedom to others, deserve it not for themselves.
Abraham Lincoln, 1856

So long as the state exists there is no freedom.
When there is freedom there will be no state.
Vladimir Ilich Lenin, *The State and Revolution*

All free men, wherever they may live, are citizens
of Berlin. And therefore, as a free man, I take
pride in the words Ich bin ein Berliner.
John F. Kennedy, West Berlin, 1963

I cannot and will not give any undertaking at a
time when I, and you, the people, are not free.
Your freedom and mine cannot be separated.
Nelson Mandela, South African lawyer and politician,
1985

We look forward to a world founded upon four
essential human freedoms. The first is freedom of
speech and expression – everywhere in the world.
The second is freedom of every person to worship
God in his own way – everywhere in the world.
The third is freedom from want – everywhere in
the world. The fourth is freedom from fear –
anywhere in the world.
Franklin D. Roosevelt, 1941

The tree of liberty must be refreshed from time to
time with the blood of patriots and tyrants. It is its
natural manure.
Thomas Jefferson

FRIENDSHIP

I always thought that Nigel [Lawson] and I were
good friends.
Prof. Alan Walters, economist, following the resignation
of Nigel Lawson after Margaret Thatcher refused to
dispense with Walters' services

Friends who knew him in Grimsby will be sorry to
hear.
Irene Lamont, mother of Norman, explaining to a local
paper why she was telling them that her son had resigned
as Chancellor of the Exchequer, 1993.

This is a sacking dressed up as a reshuffle.
Paddy Ashdown, referring to the resignation of the Chancellor, 1993

I knew him as plain David Waddington, Tory MP. I never expected to see him in a big white hat with feathers. Unlike Chris Patten, he obviously loves the uniform.
Diane Abbott, Labour MP, on seeing David Waddington, Bermuda's new governor, in his full regalia when she visited the colony

If ever I have trouble with the Communists in my country, I pick up the telephone and get on to my friend Stalin.
Eduard Benes (1884-1948), Czechoslovak National Socialist politician President, 1935-38 and 1946-48

THE FUTURE

Our task now is not to fix the blame for the past, but to fix the course for the future.
John F. Kennedy

That is a good question for you to ask, not a wise question for me to answer.
Anthony Eden, British statesman, when asked what effect Stalin's death would have on international affairs, 1953

You can trust us to wake up every day remembering the people we saw in the bus trips, the people we touched at the rallies, the people who had never voted before, the people who hadn't voted in 20 years, the people who'd never voted for a Democrat, the people who had given up hope, all of them saying we want our future back.
President Bill Clinton, after being elected to office

He has no place in the Party. He has no future in Parliament. He has no place, for Parliament is a generous place; democracy a generous thing. May I suggest he pursues his alternative career and conducts orchestras, since he does not know how to conduct himself.
Nicholas Fairbairn, of Edward Heath

Old politicians never die, they simply wade away.
Malcolm Rifkind, of John Stonehouse

He outlived the future by ten years and his past by more than twenty.
Sir Winston Churchill, of Lord Roseberry

In the last analysis it is our conception of death which decides our answers to all the questions that life puts to us.
Dag Hammarskjold (1905-61), Secretary General of the United Nations, 1951-61

I am going to visit all the countries of the world, eat all the food in the world, drink all the drink and make love, I hope, to all the women in the world.
   Maybe then get a good night's sleep.
Brian Keenan, Irish hostage, 1990, on his arrival in Dublin after being held hostage in Beirut

GOBBLEDYGOOK

I wouldn't want to mislead you by doing other than saying however easy it would be for me to answer the question you have asked, it is not fair for me to go further than I have. And I would not read too much into that.
Ian McDonald, Ministry of Defence spokesman, 1982

As I interpret the President, we're now at the end of the beginning of the upturn of the downturn.
John F. Kennedy, when Senator

You know, if an orange and an apple went into conference consultations, it might come out a pear.
Ronald Reagan

All candidates of the Natural Law Party have demonstrated greater orderliness of brain functioning, as indicated by increased EEG coherence, and greater command of Natural Law indicated by their improved mind-body coordination in their achievement of Yogic Flying. We recommend that the voters of each constituency demand comparative brain functioning analysis from the candidates of other parties.
Natural Law Party Manifesto, 1992

To the man in the street, a number of people he has barely heard of are replaced by a number of people he has never heard of.
David Mellor MP, discussing the Cabinet reshuffle, 1993

GOVERNMENT

A government which robs Peter to pay Paul can always depend on the support of Paul.
George Bernard Shaw, Everybody's Political What's What?, 1944

Government is an association of men who do violence to the rest of us.
Leo Tolstoy (1828-1910), writer and philosopher

All I want is the same thing you want. To have a nation with a government that is as good and honest and decent and competent and compassionate and as filled with love as are the American people.
Jimmy Carter, 1976

No Government can be long secure without a formidable Opposition.
Benjamin Disraeli, 1844

Governments never learn. Only people learn.
Milton Friedman, American economist, 1980

In rivers and bad governments the lightest things swim at the top.
Benjamin Franklin, Poor Richard's Almanack, 1754

Those who bear equally the burdens of
government should equally participate of its
benefits.
Thomas Jefferson, 1775

No man is good enough to govern another man
without the other's consent.
Abraham Lincoln, 1854

There can be hope only for a society which acts as
one big family, and not as many separate ones.
Anwar al-Sadat (1918-81), President of Egypt, 1978

A government that is big enough to give you all
you want is big enough to take it all away.
Barry Goldwater, US politician, quoted in *Bachman's
Book of Freedom Quotations*

This island is almost made of coal and surrounded
by fish. Only an organising genius could produce a
shortage of coal and fish in Great Britain at the
same time.
Aneurin Bevan, 1945

Government is the only known vessel that leaks
from the top.
James Reston, American journalist

Government is the political representative of
natural equilibrium, of custom of inertia; it is by
no means a representative of reason.
George Santayana (1863-1952), Spanish philosopher,
poet and novelist

In all that the people can individually do well for
themselves, government ought not to interfere.
Abraham Lincoln

The best minds are not in government. If any
were, business would hire them away.
Ronald Reagan

Go back to your constituencies and prepare for
government!
David Steel, British politician, joint head of the SDP-
Liberal Alliance, 1985

I sense that the British electorate is now itching to break out once and for all from the discredited strait-jacket of the past.
David Steel, 1987

GREEN ISSUES

Nobody will want to work for a company with a ropey reputation on the environment.
Chris Patten MP, then Secretary of State for the Environment, 1990

Supermarkets are absolutely ungreen. Many leading business people . . . are revelling in the opportunity to put new ranges on the market with 'eco-friendly' flashes and a 20 per cent mark-up.
John Button, author and Green Party candidate, 1989

Eighty per cent of pollution is caused by plants and trees.
Ronald Reagan

HEALTH

Take the wife.
Edwina Currie MP, then Junior Health Minister, advising businessmen travelling abroad on how to avoid catching AIDS, 1987

Those who prate about Blimpish patriotism in the mode of Margaret Thatcher are also the ones who will take millions off the caring services of this country.
Neil Kinnock, 1983

Mrs Thatcher took a chopper
Slashed Health Welfare good and proper,
Saying as she did so, 'Super!
After all – there's always BUPA.'
Stanley J. Sharples, New Statesman, 1984

I have lost 10 per cent of my bodyweight, so there is 10 per cent less of me to annoy people and I feel much better.
Edwina Currie MP, on becoming parliamentary slimmer of the year, 1993

We did it at the governor's mansion. We tried not to be too harsh about it.
   The big issue about health is so paramount to me that I don't think we should permit smoking.
Hillary Clinton, banning smoking from all public rooms, family quarters and offices at the White House, 1993

I stay in marvellous shape. I worry it off.
Nancy Reagan

I am sorry to have to say that . . . this was not entirely accurate.
Jeremy Hanley, Defence Minister, admitting misleading the Commons over the health warning about the depleted uranium used by Gulf War troops

Consultants can be downright rude and abusive to patients and some of them are no better than local football yobs.
Ronnie Campbell MP, attacking hospital consultants, 1993

Smoking is a dying habit.
Virginia Bottomley MP, Minister of Health, 1993

HOUSE OF COMMONS

. . . Like playing squash with a dish of scrambled eggs.
Harold Nicolson, on debating with Nancy Astor in the House of Commons, 1943

There are three golden rules for Parliamentary speakers: 'Stand up. Speak up. Shut up.'
J. W. Lowther, Speaker of the House of Commons, 1919

I do not know what the Right Hon. Lady the Minister for Education [Miss Florence Horsburgh] is grinning at. I was told by one of my Hon. friends this afternoon that this is a face which has sunk a thousand scholarships.
Aneurin Bevan, on cuts in the Education budget, House of Commons, 1953

As we had great interests there and also on general grounds, I thought that it would be a good thing to have diplomatic representation. But if you recognise anyone, it does not mean that you like him. We all, for instance, recognise the Right Hon. Gentleman the Member of Ebbw Vale [Aneurin Bevan].
Sir Winston Churchill, speech on the recognition of Communist China, House of Commons, 1952

. . . a Bill to make attendance at the House of Commons compulsory has been passed by three votes to two.
To England with Love, 1967

I have nothing against Hampstead. I used to live there myself when I was an intellectual. I gave that up when I became Leader of the House.
Norman St John-Stevas, 1980

Only people who look dull ever get into the House of Commons, and only people who are dull ever succeed there.
Oscar Wilde, *An Ideal Husband,* 1895

They see the House of Commons as a political soap opera, complete with its Dirty Dens, JRs and Kylie Minogues – good for entertainment, but not of much real relevance to their lives.
Paddy Ashdown, on the public perception of politicians, 1993

A Palace of Illogicalities.
Lord George Brown, *In My Way,* 1971

It is nine-tenths utter boredom.
Bernard Weatherill, on the role of 'Speaker of the House'

It is not so much a gentleman's club as a boys' boarding school.
Shirley Williams

This place is a ridiculous madhouse seemingly invented by Kafka. You start work at 2.30 in the afternoon and you finish at 10 at night. It is an institution deliberately designed to give MPs the earliest possible heart attack, to deny them any social life and to smash up their marriages.
Paddy Ashdown, Liberal Party Leader, *Living* Magazine interview

If one cannot come to the House of Commons and tell them what is wrong with the system, if one cannot speak in this place, not about innocence or guilt, not about trials, not about sub judice, but what is wrong with the system, then what is the point of being here?
Michael Mates MP, alleging attempts by the Serious Fraud office to pervert the course of justice

HOUSE OF LORDS

The House of Lords is a model of how to care for the elderly.
Frank Field, Labour MP, 1981

The House of Lords is not the watchdog of the constitution: it is Mr Balfour's poodle. It fetches and carries for him. It barks for him. It bites anybody that he sets it on to!
David Lloyd George, 1908

The House of Lords is like a glass of champagne that has stood for five days.
Clement Attlee

You can't say: 'The noble and gallant Lord is a silly old fool.' It just wouldn't sound right.
Lady Phillips, 1967

The House of Lords is a perfect eventide home.
Lady Stocks, 1970 (attrib.)

The cure for admiring the House of Lords is to go and look at it.
Walter Bagehot, English historian

It was but a few weeks since he had taken his seat in the Lords; and this afternoon, for want of anything better to do, he strayed in.
Max Beerbohm, Zuleika Dobson, 1911

The House of Lords is the British Outer Mongolia for retired politicians.
Tony Benn, 1962

The House of Lords is the only club in the world where the proprietor pays for the drinks.
Michael Foot

Five hundred men, ordinary men, chosen accidentally from among the unemployed.
David Lloyd George

The House of Lords has a value – it is good evidence of life after death.
Lord Soper, 1978

We in the House of Lords are never in touch with public opinion. That makes us a civilised body.
Oscar Wilde, A Woman of No Importance, 1893

IDEALISM

He reminds me of King Canute.
Cyril Smith, of Nigel Lawson

I watch his smart-alec manner and his British
clothes and that New Dealism, everlasting New
Dealism in everything he says and does, and I
want to shout, 'Get out, get out. You stand for
everything that has been wrong with the United
States for years.'
John Adams, of Dean Acheson

IMAGE

John Major thinks this man is a serious political
figure.
Alastair Campbell, 1992, of Jeffrey Archer

I'd rate him nine out of ten. But he loses a point
because of the shifty way he touches his nose.
Dr Michael Durtnard, Chiropractor, 1992, of Paddy
Ashdown

She looks like a woman resigned to walk home
alone to an empty bedsit after Grab-a-Granny
night at the local disco.
Richard Littlejohn, The Sun, 1992, of Acting Leader of
the Labour Party, Margaret Beckett

A thug in twin-set and pearls.
Anne Robinson, The Daily Mirror, 1992, of Virginia
Bottomley, Health Minister

She has done for our party what King Herod did
for babysitting.
Andrew MacKay, of Edwina Currie

He created the impression of being rather dated,
rather fuddy-duddy, rather aristocratic, indifferent
in health and altogether too well-mannered for
politics in the age of Harold Wilson.
Sir Gerald Nabarro, 1963, of Sir Alec Douglas-Home,
Conservative MP and Prime Minister (1963-64)

He is a mixture of Hamlet, Rasputin and Tommy Cooper.
Denis Healey, of Keith Joseph

Gary Hart is just Jerry Brown without the fruit flies.
Robert Strauss

Hart is Kennedy typed on the eighth carbon.
Lance Morrow, of Gary Hart, 1987

INCOMPETENCE

A good mayor of Birmingham in an off-year.
David Lloyd George, of Neville Chamberlain

He was not a good judge of men, nor had he enough experience to temper his enthusiasm. He was a political goose.
Clement Attlee, of Sir Stafford Cripps

His Accidency.
Theodore Roosevelt, of Grover Cleveland

Foster Dulles is the only case I know of a bull who carries a china shop with him.
Sir Winston Churchill

An unmistakable fog of political incompetence is beginning to form around the White House.
The New York Times, on Bill Clinton, 1993

INDECISION

He lies on his back with his legs waggling in the air. I've never heard such a weak-kneed response.
Anthony Beaumont-Dark, of Kenneth Baker

He has half a dozen solutions to any problem and one of them is right – the trouble is he does not know which it is.
David Lloyd George, of Sir Winston Churchill

He has shifted his bottom along the fence, but he's still sitting on it.
Paddy Ashdown, 1992, of Neil Kinnock

Karaoke Kinnock, the man who'll sing any song you want him to.
Ian Lang, 1992

The chameleon of politics consistent only in his inconsistency.
John Major, of Neil Kinnock, 1992

We know what happens to people who stay in the middle of the road. They get run over.
Aneurin Bevan, 1953

INDUSTRY

Manufacturing wealth is not the be-all and end-all of life. It's wealth creation that counts. That's sometimes done by manufacturing and sometimes done by service sector and other activities.
Lord Young of Graffham, former Secretary of State for Trade and Industry, *The Amstrad Story,* 1990

This could fairly be described as the most helpless Government in the whole history of government. It arouses compassion.
Lord Longford, 1993

His knowledge of industry could be accommodated on the back of a four-penny stamp.
Sir Gerald Nabarro, of Michael Foot

As Trade and Industry Secretary he must have one of the easiest jobs around because there's not much trade and very little industry.
Member of *Question Time* audience, 1992

INFLATION

Inflation is the parent of unemployment and the unseen robber of those who have saved.
Margaret Thatcher, 1980

Inflation is a disease of money.
Nigel Lawson MP, 1989

Inflation is as violent as a mugger, as frightening as an armed robber and as deadly as a hit man.
Ronald Reagan

Mrs Thatcher has been promising zero inflation for 11 years. What she did not say was that she would put a one before the zero.
Neil Kinnock MP, commenting on the rise of inflation to 10.6 per cent, 1990

Even after the revolution we didn't confiscate current accounts.
Fidel Castro, commenting on President Fernando Collor's anti-inflation measures in Brazil, 1990

Inflation in the '60s was a nuisance to be endured, like varicose veins or French foreign policy.
Bernard Levin, British journalist, *The Pendulum Years*

In the next Parliament we aim to eliminate inflation altogether.
Nigel Lawson MP, then Chancellor of the Exchequer, 1986

The sharp deterioration has now come to an end.
Nigel Lawson MP, then Chancellor of the Exchequer, on the trade figures, 1989

INTELLECT

Not dead. But the candle in that great turnip has gone out.
Sir Winston Churchill, of Stanley Baldwin

That not very bright Mr Kinnock, the famous Welsh windbag.
Anthony King, *The Daily Telegraph*, 1992

Absolutely ghastly. The trouble with brains is they don't breed common sense.
Anthony Beaumont-Dark, 1992

Here, indeed, was his one really notable talent. He slept more than any other President, whether by day or by night. Nero fiddled, but Coolidge snored. He had no ideas and he was not a nuisance.
H. L. Mencken, *American Mercury,* 1933

It was hard to listen to Goldwater and realise that a man could be half Jewish and yet sometimes appear twice as dense as the normal gentile.
I. F. Stone, 1968, of Barry Goldwater

An empty suit that goes to funerals and plays golf.
H. Ross Perot, 1992, of J. Danforth (Dan) Quayle

I have never met a man who was both intelligent and a Peronist.
Jorge Luis Borges, of Juan Peron, President of Argentina

THE LABOUR PARTY

The 1984 Labour Party Conference last night exceeded its wildest expectations of its traditionally wild behaviour. In a pent-up frenzy of balloting . . . it managed to vote against everything in sight. This has long been the position of many of the comrades where real life is concerned. But it has never been official party policy up to now, the preferred compromise being to vote in favour of conflicting things.
Michael White, 1984

[Minister of Technology, Anthony Wedgwood] Benn flung himself into the '60s technology with the enthusiasm (not to say language) of a newly enrolled Boy Scout demonstrating knot-tying to his indulgent parents.
Bernard Levin, *The Pendulum Years,* 1970

The Labour Party is not dead, just brain dead.
Norman Tebbit

The Labour Party is like a stage-coach. If you rattle along at great speed everybody inside is too exhilarated or too seasick to cause any trouble. But if you stop, everybody gets out and argues about where to go next.
Harold Wilson

I do not often attack the Labour Party. They do it so well themselves.
Edward Heath, 1973

They are not fit to manage a whelk stall.
Winston Churchill (attrib.)

That bunch of rootless intellectuals, alien Jews and international pederasts who call themselves the Labour Party.
Alan Bennett, Forty Years On, 1968

The Socialist movement in England has never been remarkable for the possession of first-class brains.
Lord Birkenhead

What a genius the Labour Party has for cutting itself in half and letting the two parts writhe in public.
Cassandra, The Daily Mirror

A Labour Government is government of the duds, by the duds and for the duds.
Sir Winston Churchill

The Socialist dream is no longer Utopia, but Queutopia.
Sir Winston Churchill, on continued rationing under Labour

The idea that there is a model Labour voter, a blue-collar council house tenant who belongs to a union and has 2.4 children, a five-year-old car and a holiday in Blackpool, is patronising and politically immature.
Neil Kinnock, 1986

The American declaration of Independence said 'All men are created equal', but the British Socialist party says 'All men shall be kept equal'.
Bryan Gould, 1992

It's no use saying that the Labour Government works if one and a half million [unemployed] do not.
Jo Haines, 1977

The things that divide the Party are much greater than the things that unite them.
Frank Johnson, 1984

Scotland needs the Labour Party as much as Sicily needs the Mafia.
Malcolm Rifkind, 1992

The grotesque chaos of a Labour Council – a Labour Council – hiring taxis to scuttle around a city handing out redundancy notices to its own workers.
Neil Kinnock, attacking militant members in Liverpool, 1985

A dodgy leader of a dodgy party, not quite 100p to the pound.
Michael Heseltine, 1992, of Neil Kinnock and the Labour Party

LACK OF JUDGMENT

He has an infallible knack for getting the wrong end of every stick.
Nigel Lawson, of Neil Kinnock

LAW AND ORDER

Necessity has no law; I know some attorneys of the same.
Benjamin Franklin

It is the trade of lawyers to question everything, yield to nothing, and to talk by the hour.
Thomas Jefferson

Discourage litigation. Persuade your neighbour to compromise whenever you can. As a peacemaker the lawyer has a superior opportunity of being a good man. There will still be business enough.
Abraham Lincoln

I believe that people would be alive today if there were a death penalty.
Nancy Reagan

I can't see that it's wrong to give him a little legal experience before he goes out to practise law.
John F. Kennedy, on being criticised for making his brother Robert Attorney General

God works wonders now and then. Behold! A lawyer, an honest man.
Benjamin Franklin, American statesman (1706-90)

I believe we must make it absolutely clear for law-abiding citizens that it is their interests we are going to look after.
Margaret Thatcher, 1979

. . . the challenge for the '90s is to step up the fight against lawlessness and violence so that our citizens are free from fear.
John Major, party manifesto, 1992

I have my own Parkinson's Law: in politics people give you what they think you deserve and deny you what they think you want.
Cecil (later Lord) Parkinson MP

People of 16 can engage in what may be the biggest lottery in life by getting married. Why on earth should they not be allowed to buy lottery tickets?
John Maxton, Labour MP

By our readiness to allow arms to be purchased at will and fired at whim, we have created an atmosphere in which violence and hatred have become popular pastimes.
Martin Luther King Jr

What in the name of conscience will it take to pass a truly effective gun-control law? Now in this new hour of tragedy, let us spell out our grief in constructive action.
Lyndon B. Johnson

With all the violence and murder and killings we've had in the United States, I think you will agree that we must keep firearms from people who have no business with guns.
Robert F. Kennedy, five days before his assassination, 1968

We prefer world law in the age of self-determination – we reject world war in the age of mass extermination.
John F. Kennedy

From 6.45 a.m. to lights out at 9.30 p.m. life will be conducted at a brisk tempo. Much greater emphasis will be put on hard and constructive activities, on discipline and tidiness, on self-respect and respect for those in authority.
William Whitelaw, Home Secretary, announcing 'short, sharp, shock' treatment for young offenders, 1979

The Government's general policies of strengthening the police and the emphasis on law and order must also make a contribution to tackling this problem.
Norman Fowler, Transport Secretary, on violence on trains, 1980

The two offences of which people of all ages are most fearful are violent street crime and burglary. Efforts against these two crimes must be targeted to make the best possible use of the available intelligence and skilled detective powers.
Sir Leon Brittan, Home Secretary, 1983

Under this Government those who prey on their fellow citizens do so at their peril.
Sir Leon Brittan, 1984

The low price and high purity of the drugs being peddled on London streets are grim indications of the amount of drugs still reaching this country and there are no signs of crack being widely used in London yet.
Douglas Hurd, Home Secretary, 1986

There are three prongs to our anti-crime drive: stronger sentences, more police on the beat and prevention.
John Patten, 1987

The family is our first defence against crime. For too long in this country we have pushed parental responsibility to the sidelines.
Douglas Hurd, Home Secretary, 1989

Sentences served should be much closer to sentences passed.
Lord Waddington, Home Secretary, 1989

The vast majority of offences are committed not by determined professionals but by dishonest youngsters left to their own devices.
Lord Waddington, Home Secretary, 1990

Crime is always in the news. Crime prevention doesn't feature so often in the headlines but in the last 10 years, and in the last five particularly, we have put crime prevention on the agenda for every police force, every local authority, every housing association, every car manufacturer and insurer, and on the personal agenda of many millions of ordinary people.
Kenneth Baker, Home Secretary, 1991

No Conservative government has ever accepted that parts of our inner-cities might become no-go areas for the rule of law.
Kenneth Baker, Home Secretary, 1991

We want to make quite sure that it's effective and tough and the Bill is now being drafted.
Kenneth Baker, Home Secretary, on measures to tackle joy riding, 1991

It is no use peddling the idea that unemployment and crime are the Government's fault and opportunities are restricted by, for instance, lack of child care or racism. I see the growth of a so-called underclass as the most formidable challenge to a secure and civilised way of life throughout the developed world.
Kenneth Clarke, Home Secretary, 1992

We have so reduced the power of the courts to lock up children – for basically good reasons – we now have a handful of young people we cannot really cope with.
Kenneth Clarke, Home Secretary, 1993

THE LIBERAL PARTY

A Liberal . . . One who has both feet planted
firmly in the air.
Adlai Stevenson

It is easy for the Liberals to say that something
should be done on a bigger scale. They never have
to do these things.
Patrick Gordon Walker, Labour Minister, 1967

Liberals are variously described as limousine,
double-domed, screaming, knee-jerk, professional
and 'bleeding heart'.
William Safire, The New Language of Politics, 1968

Basically the Liberal Party is divided between
wispy beards and others. Wispy beards . . . wear
T-shirts with slogans on, usually faintly dated, e.g.
'The Only Safe Fast Breeder is a Rabbit'. They
tend to have ill-fitting jeans, and those shoes which
look like Cornish Pasties. They have briefcases
stuffed with documents, chiefly about community
politics, nuclear power and ecology. They drink
real ale.
Simon Hoggart, On The House, 1981

As usual the Liberals offer a mixture of sound and
original ideas. Unfortunately, none of the sound
ideas is original and none of the original ideas is
sound.
Harold Macmillan, 1961

. . . the small troupe of exhibitionists, failed
vaudeville artists, juicy young Boy Scouts and
degenerate old voluptuaries which is the Liberal
Party.
Auberon Waugh, writer, *Private Eye*

If God had been a Liberal, we wouldn't have had
the ten commandments – we'd have the ten
suggestions.
Malcolm Bradbury

A man who leaves the room when the fight begins.
Heywood C. Broun

A person who understands everything but the people who don't understand him.
Lenny Bruce

The Liberals are the flying saucers of politics. No one can make head nor tail of them and they never are twice seen in the same place.
John G. Diefenbaker (1895-1979), Canadian Conservative politician, 1962

A power worshipper without the power.
George Orwell

I can remember way back when a liberal was one who was generous with his own money.
Will Rogers

The truth is that the Liberals do not want to abolish the House of Lords when it opposes the people – but wish to abolish the people when they oppose the Liberal Party.
Lord Birkenhead

The Liberal Government has turned its back on the country and now has the impertinence to claim the country is behind it.
Lord Birkenhead

Don't vote for Paddy LETdown . . . There is one party you should scrap off the slate in this election. That's Paddy Ashdown and his prigs. Captain Ashdown hasn't got enough 'trained troops' to run the taps in a toilet.
The Daily Star, 1992

A one-man band who has transformed a party without a leader into a leader without a party . . . And he was a leader with more answers than there were questions, and more news conferences than there were newspapers.
Michael Heseltine, on Paddy Ashdown, 1992

THE LIBERAL-
DEMOCRATIC PARTY
(L D P)

Woolly-hatted, muesli-eating, Tory lickspittles.
Tony Banks MP

To expect the Liberals to control Labour would be
like asking Dad's Army to retrain the Mongol
hordes.
Douglas Hurd, 1992

One week before the election, the Labour Party
start cuddling up to the Liberal-Democrats for
support. It is like leaning on candy-floss.
John Major, 1992

The Liberal-Democrats are a Trojan horse to the
Labour Party.
John Major, 1992

The Liberal-Democrats couldn't survive a
moment's scrutiny of their policies. At local level
they back four routes for a by-pass – North,
South, East and West. At national level, they are
just as bad.
Chris Patten, 1992

Liberals are Enid Blyton Socialists – a dustbin for
undecided votes.
Norman Tebbit

They have a new colour. They call it gold; it looks
like yellow to me.
Margaret Thatcher

L I E S

A lie can be half-way round the world before the
truth has got its boots on.
James Callaghan, 1976

A lie is an abomination unto the Lord and a very
present help in trouble.
Adlai Stevenson, 1951

I offer my opponents a bargain: if they will stop
telling falsehoods about us, I will stop telling the
truth about them.
Adlai Stevenson, during the presidential campaign, 1952

The only major politician in the country who can
be labelled 'liar' without fear of libel.
Joseph and Stewart Alsop, 1953, of Senator Joseph
McCarthy

MARXISM

The Marxist analysis has got nothing to do with
what happened in Stalin's Russia: it's like blaming
Jesus Christ for the Inquisition in Spain.
Tony Benn

All I know is I'm not a Marxist.
Karl Marx

Marxism is essentially a product of a bourgeois
mind.
J. A. Schumpeter (1883-1950), American economist

THE MEDIA

The man who never looks into a newspaper is
better informed than he who reads them, inasmuch
as he who knows nothing is nearer to truth than
he whose mind is filled with falsehoods and errors.
Thomas Jefferson, 1807

On the whole I would not say that our Press is
obscene. I would say that it trembles on the brink
of obscenity.
Lord Longford, 1963

If I blow my nose they would say I'm trying to
spread germ warfare.
Ken Livingstone, of the *Daily Mail,* 1992

Newspapers too thick, lavatory paper too thin.
Sir Winston Churchill, on returning from New York

I shall resist the temptation to dwell on the golden age of the '50s and '60s when I was a financial journalist. But I must say I am struck by the modern obsession with inevitably speculative forecasts of the short-term future, at the expense of informing the reader about what is actually happening in the present.
Nigel Lawson, then Chancellor of the Exchequer, 1984

I think we've been treated to a dose of the sort of sanctimonious humbug which is characteristic of sections of the British press. It is the politics of envy and an awful lot of humbug. Everybody knows that people get paid all different salaries, that newspaper editors don't do all that badly, but it's a sort of nauseating form of demagoguery.
Nigel Lawson, responding to criticism of his appointment to highly paid directorships following his resignation as Chancellor, 1990

I cheered like mad when a couple of papers got clobbered with damages of half a million pounds.
Clive Soley, Labour MP, on the libel laws, 1993

If we are looking to the current breed of newspaper owners and editors properly to safeguard press freedom, we are wasting our time.
Robin Corbett, Labour MP, 1993

Politicians who complain about the media are like ships' captains who complain about the sea.
Enoch Powell (attrib.)

Politicians are always deeply shocked to see anything in the newspapers which is not about themselves or their piffling preoccupations, but very few people, in fact, are remotely interested in either.
Auberon Waugh, 1984

Interviewing politicians can be like nailing custard to the wall.
John Humphrys, BBC interviewer

Whenever people are well informed they can be trusted with their own government.
Thomas Jefferson

We live under a government of men and morning newspapers.
Wendell Phillips (1811-84), American orator

No government ought to be without censors; and where the press is free none ever will.
Thomas Jefferson

You know very well that whether you are on page one or page thirty depends on whether they fear you. It is just as simple as that.
Richard Nixon

The men with the muck-rake are often indispensable to the well-being of society, but only if they know when to stop raking the muck.
Theodore Roosevelt

One gets the impression from the popular Press that rape has become the British national pastime.
Lord Wigoder, British barrister and Liberal politician

Generally speaking, the Press lives on disaster.
Clement Attlee

I'm sure if I have any plans, the Press will inform me.
Arthur Scargill

I got to know Ike's plumbing like the back of my hand. I could walk around his innards in the dark.
Cassandra, British journalist

Almost from the moment the horror occurred, television changed. It was no longer a small box containing entertainment, news and sports; suddenly, it was a window opening onto violently unpredictable life in Washington and in Dallas, where a President had been assassinated.
Newsweek, on coverage of John F. Kennedy's assassination, 1963

You have a great future in television.
Producer of *A Kick in the Ballots,* to Charles Kennedy MP, who chairs the television quiz programme, 1993

It's part of the strategy for cutting budget deficits. All kinds of new commercial projects are currently under discussion.
A Pentagon source, referring to a campaign of space advertising being planned by Bill Clinton, 1993

What the proprietorship of these newspapers is aiming at is power without responsibility – the prerogative of the harlot through the ages.
Stanley Baldwin, of Lord Beaverbrook

I feel sorry for them [the press] because they should recognise that to the extent they allow their own hatreds to consume them, they will lose the rationality which is the mark of a civilised man.
Richard Nixon to Rabbi Korff

To hell with them. When history is written they will be the sons of bitches – not I.
Harry S. Truman

You won't have Nixon to kick around anymore, gentlemen. This is my last Press Conference.
Richard Nixon at a press conference for governorship of California, 1962

An editor is one who separates the wheat from the chaff and prints the chaff.
Adlai Stevenson, The Stevenson Wit

Written by office boys for office boys.
Marquess of Salisbury (1830-1903), British statesman, on the launch of the *Daily Mail*, 1896

Jimmy, I think he should do your job and you should have done his.
Tony Benn MP to presenter Jimmy Young, when asked about Neil Kinnock, MP's Radio 2 debut

The BBC management may become international media players but they are also public servants.
Marjorie Mowlam MP, Labour Heritage Spokeswoman

MEMORIES

I was in short trousers; we had ration cards; Hitler had been dead for only seven years. They were, I remember, happy days.
John Major, on the year *The Mousetrap* opened, 1993

MILITARY

I studied dramatics under him for 12 years.
Dwight D. Eisenhower, of General Douglas MacArthur

I fired him because he wouldn't respect the authority of the President. I didn't fire him because he was a dumb son-of-a-bitch, although he was, but that's not against the law for generals. If it was, half to three-quarters of them would be in jail.
Harry S. Truman, of General Douglas MacArthur

They have a propaganda machine that is almost equal to Stalin's.
Harry S. Truman, of the Marine Corps, 1956

Traditions of the Royal Navy? I'll give you traditions of the Navy – rum, sodomy and the lash.
Sir Winston Churchill, 1939

The basic problems facing the world today are not susceptible to a military solution.
John F. Kennedy

And, as everyone knows, the army is a poor training corps for democracy, no matter how inspiring its cause.
Pierre Trudeau

MISTAKES

The greatest mistake I made was not to die in office.
Dean Acheson (1893-1971), American Democratic politician, on hearing eulogies to his successor as Secretary of State, John Foster Dulles, who died in office.

As Moses he would have mistimed his arrival at
the parting of the waves.
Austin Mitchell, of James Callaghan

Putting him in charge of industrial relations is like
appointing Dracula to take charge of the blood
transfusion service.
Eric Varley, of Norman Tebbit

MONARCHY

There is something behind the throne greater than
the King himself.
William Pitt the Elder, 1770

A monarchy is a merchant man which sails well,
but will sometimes strike on a rock, and go to the
bottom; a republic is a raft which will never sink,
but then your feet are always in the water.
Fisher Ames (1758-1808), American politician, 1795

The US Presidency is a Tudor monarchy plus
telephones.
[John] Anthony Burgess [Wilson], English born
novelist and critic, *Writers at Work,* 1977

The tourists who come to our island take in the
Monarchy along with feeding the pigeons in
Trafalgar Square.
Willie Hamilton, Scottish MP and Labour politician,
My Queen and I

Every country should have at least one King
Farouk.
Gore Vidal, 1981, of Edward Kennedy

In Prussia it is only kings who make revolutions.
Prince Otto von Bismarck (1815-1898), German
Politician, Chancellor, 1871-1890, in conversation with
Napoleon III, 1862

M O N E Y

Nobody would remember the Good Samaritan if he had only good intentions. He had money as well.
Margaret Thatcher, 1980

Make all you can, save all you can, give all you can.
Margaret Thatcher, quoting John Wesley (the founder of Methodism), 1988

Mrs Thatcher is doing for monetarism what the Boston Strangler is doing for door-to-door salesmen.
Denis Healey MP, former Chancellor of the Exchequer, 1979

I am very far from being prepared to admit that the improvement of the situation of a common police constable by giving him more money would increase the efficiency of the establishment.
Robert Peel (1788-1850), British Conservative and Prime Minister, in a letter to John Croker, 1829

Nothing is easier than spending public money. It does not appear to belong to anybody. The temptation is overwhelming to bestow it on somebody.
Calvin Coolidge

We have a very small stick and no carrots.
Boris Fyodorov, Russian Finance Minister, 1993

Phrases like 'catching up' and 'cost of living increase' which trip off the tongue of many negotiators should be on the way out. In the not too distant future, the notion of automatic pay increase must become as exceptional as it was novel a generation ago.
Sir Geoffrey Howe MP, then Chancellor of the Exchequer, 1982

Anyone who makes a lot of money quickly must be pretty crooked – honest pushing away at the grindstone never made anyone a bomb.
Mandy Rice-Davies, call-girl in British political scandal, 1963

Politics has got so expensive that it takes a lot of money even to get beat with.
Will Rogers

The charge he must answer is not that he ever arranged with the noble lords to meet around the back of a motorway service station to pick up his bung and hand over the gong. The charge is much more urbane. Word gets around that the chances of a peerage or knighthood are multiplied by generous donations.
Robin Cook, Labour industry spokesman, addressing Sir Norman Fowler in the Commons on the subject of Party funding, 1992

Pennies do not come from heaven. They have to be earned here on earth.
Margaret Thatcher, 1982

His idea of policy is to spend, spend, spend. He is the Viv Nicholson of politics.
John Major, of Michael Foot, Labour Party leader (1980-83)

NATIONALISATION AND PRIVATISATION

Selling the family silver.
Harold Macmillan, referring to privatisation of profitable nationalised industries, 1986

Dr Johnson could have said: when you know you are going to be privatised, it concentrates the mind wonderfully.
Margaret Thatcher, 1986

Successful businessmen do not take jobs in nationalised industries.
Margaret Thatcher, reported comment to Sir Peter Parker, then chairman, British Rail, 1982

First all the Georgian silver goes, and then that nice furniture that used to be in the salon. Then the Canalettos go.
Lord Stockton, on privatisation, 1985

We'll find it very difficult to explain to the voters that simply by taking over Marks & Spencer we can make it as efficient as the Co-op.
Harold Wilson, former Labour Prime Minister, 1973

From the days when the miners thought they owned the government to the day when every miner owns part of his own mine – that's the British revolution.
Cecil Parkinson MP, then Secretary of State for Energy, 1988

The spread of personal ownership is in harmony with the deepest instincts of the British people. Few changes have done more to create one nation.
Nigel Lawson MP, 1988

This is £21.8 million down the plughole. I find the water commercials quite outrageous – they seem to be gratuitously telling us that we never had water until people thought about privatising it.
Anthony Beaumont-Dark MP, on the amount of money being spent on advertising the privatisation of water, 1989

John Redwood's zeal for privatisation will go down like a rat sandwich.
Ieuan Wyn Jones, Plaid Cymru MP, of the newly appointed Welsh Secretary, 1993

Tory rebellions are a bit like tooth fairies – believe in them when you see them.
Brian Wilson, Labour transport spokesman, on backbench opposition to rail privatisation plans

NATIONALISM

Italy will do it alone.
Charles Albert (1798-1849), King of Piedmont, referring to the movement to liberate and unify Italy, 1848

A balanced state of well-modulated dissatisfaction.
Eduard, Count von Taaffe (1833-94), Austrian Prime Minister referring to his policy towards nationalistic tensions within the Austro-Hungarian Empire

Germany will either be a world power or will not be at all.
Adolf Hitler, Mein Kampf

After 15 years of work I have achieved, as a common German soldier and merely with my fanatical will-power, the unity of the German nation, and have freed it from the death sentence of Versailles.
Adolf Hitler, 1941

Nations whose nationalism is destroyed are subject to ruin.
Colonel Muammar Gaddafi

If I were an American, as I am an Englishman, while a foreign troop was landed in my country, I never would lay down my arms, never – never – never!
William Pitt, the Elder, 1777

When it comes to constitutional issues in Wales, we trust Neil Kinnock about as far as we could drop-kick him.
Dafydd Wigley, Plaid Cymru, 1992

NATIONS

I found there a country with 32 religions and only one sauce.
Talleyrand (1754-1838), French politician, referring to America

Italy is a geographical expression.
Clement Metternich (1773-1859), Austrian diplomat and Chancellor, 1847

The Empire is a Commonwealth of Nations.
Earl of Rosebery, British statesman, 1884

One step forward, two steps back . . . It happens in the lives of individuals, and it happens in the history of nations and in the development of parties.
Vladimir Ilich Lenin, One Step Forward, Two Steps Back

India is no more a political personality than
Europe. India is a geographical term. It is no more
a united nation than the equator.
Sir Winston Churchill, 1931

THE NUCLEAR AGE

The atom bomb is a paper tiger which the United
States reactionaries use to scare people.
Mao Tse-Tung, 1946

No country without an atomic bomb could
properly consider itself independent.
Charles de Gaulle, 1968

The atom bomb was no 'great decision' . . . It was
merely another powerful weapon in the arsenal of
righteousness.
Harry S. Truman

I would die for my country . . . but I would not let
my country die for me.
Neil Kinnock, 1987

OBSCENITIES

On one famous occasion, the Prime Minister was
accused of 'mouthing' the ultimate obscenity in the
House. Inspiration striking, Trudeau insisted that
the actual phrase was 'Fuddle-duddle!'
Anon., of Pierre Trudeau

Filthy Story-Teller, Despot, Liar, Thief, Braggart,
Buffoon, Usurper, Monster, Ignoramus Abe, Old
Scoundrel, Perjurer, Robber, Swindler, Tyrant,
Field-Butcher, Land-Pirate.
Harper's Weekly, on Lincoln

I do not mind the Liberals, still less do I mind the Country Party, calling me a bastard. In some circumstances I am only doing my job if they do. But I hope you will not publicly call me a bastard, as some bastards in the Caucus have.
Gough Whitlam, Australian statesman, in a speech to the Australian Labour Party, 1974

We don't want three more of the bastards out there spreading poison.
John Major, explaining why he didn't sack the Eurosceptic Ministers, 1993

Every Prime Minister should have a Willie.
Margaret Thatcher, of her Deputy, Lord Whitelaw, *Sunday Times*

To listen to some people in politics; you'd think 'nice' was a four-letter word.
Sir David Steel, Party Political Broadcast, 1987

He spoke the truth. He should not apologise.
Edward Heath, on John Major's 'Bastards' comment

OPINION

Public opinion in this country is everything.
Abraham Lincoln

I often think how much easier the world would have been to manage if Herr Hitler and Signor Mussolini had been at Oxford.
Viscount Halifax (1881-1959), British politician, 1937

The crafty, cold-blooded, black-hearted Italian.
Sir Winston Churchill, British statesman, referring to Benito Mussolini, 1941

Not a gentleman; dresses too well.
Bertrand Russell, British philosopher, referring to Anthony Eden

McCarthyism is Americanism with its sleeves rolled.
Joseph McCarthy (1908-57), US Senator, notorious as the instigator of investigations of supposed communists, 1952

It's not that I don't have opinions, rather than I'm paid not to think aloud.
Yitzhak Navon, Israeli politician

I never offered an opinion till I was 60, and then it was one which had been in our family for a century.
Benjamin Disraeli

I thought he was a young man of promise; but it appears he was a young man of promises.
Arthur Balfour (1848-1930), British statesman, of Winston Churchill on his entry into politics, 1899

Prime Minister Major seems to have an instinct for making a beeline towards the brink of political disaster.
The Washington Post, 1990

We had no use for the policy of the Gospels: if someone slaps you, just turn the other cheek. We had shown that anyone who slapped us on our cheek would get his head kicked off.
Nikita Khrushchev (1894-1971), Soviet statesman, *Khrushchev Remembers*

London is a splendid place to live for those who can get out of it.
Lord Balfour of Burleigh, 1944

I don't give a tuppenny hoot.
John Major, when asked about his attitude to class

OPPORTUNITY

Opportunity is the great bawd.
Benjamin Franklin

Next to knowing when to seize an opportunity, the most important thing in life is to know when to forego an advantage.
Benjamin Disraeli

He is the acceptable face of opportunism.
David Owen, of Roy Hattersley

It is wrong to kick John Patten when he is down.
But try to stop me.
Roy Hattersley MP, on the dismissal of the former
Education Secretary

OPTIMISM

In the next Parliament we aim to eliminate
inflation altogether.
Nigel Lawson MP, Chancellor of the Exchequer, 1986

The sharp deterioration has now come to an end.
Nigel Lawson MP, referring to the trade figures, 1989

These are not dark days; these are great days – the
greatest days our country has ever lived.
Sir Winston Churchill

Pessimism of the intellect; optimism of the will.
Antonio Gramsci (1891-1937), Italian political theorist

Government Ministers are expected at all times to
preach good news, and the introduction of realism
is not normally encouraged.
Chris Moncrieff, political editor of the Press
Association, commenting on the warning that a Tory loss
in the Christchurch by-election could accelerate a Labour
victory at the next general election, 1993

There's not a seat in the country that we could
hold at the moment.
A cabinet minister in an off-the-record quote, 1993

I'm an optimist, but an optimist who carries a
raincoat.
Harold Wilson

We can no more stop fighting the battle against
'big government' than the gardener can stop
mowing the lawn or digging out the ground elder.
John Major

OWNERSHIP

It is inconceivable that we could transform this
society without a major extension of public
ownership.
Neil Kinnock, *Marxism Today,* 1983

PARLIAMENT

Parliament is the longest running farce in the West
End.
Cyril Smith, Liberal MP, 1973

To anyone with politics in his blood, this place is
like a pub to a drunkard.
David Lloyd George, Welsh Liberal politician, of the
House of Commons

You behold a range of exhausted volcanoes.
Benjamin Disraeli, of the Front Bench

The Commons, faithful to their system, remained
in a wise and masterly inactivity.
Sir James Mackintosh (1765-1832), Scottish
philosopher

Parliament is nothing less than a big meeting of
more or less idle people.
Walter Bagehot

When we have finally stirred ourselves to hang
them all, I hope our next step will be to outlaw
political parties outside Parliament on the grounds
that, like amusement arcades, they attract all the
least desirable members of Society.
Auberon Waugh, 1984

It is said to be hard on His Majesty's Ministers to
raise objections to this proposition. For my part I
think it no more hard on His Majesty's Opposition
to compel them to take this course.
First recorded use of the phrase 'His Majesty's Opposition',
House of Commons, 27 April 1826

When I first came into Parliament, Mr Tierney, a great Whig authority, used always to say that the duty of an Opposition was very simple – it was to oppose everything, and propose nothing.
Edward Stanley (1799-1869), British Conservative Prime Minister

I dreamt that I was making a speech in the House. I woke up, and by Jove I was!
Duke of Devonshire (1833-1908), Conservative politician

I once did a season at Butlins and that was very good training for the House of Commons.
Liz Lynne, Liberal Democrat MP, 1993

The House of Lords is the British Outer Mongolia for retired politicians.
Tony Benn, British politician, 1962

I had better recall before someone else does, that I said on one occasion that all was fair in love, war and parliamentary procedure.
Michael Foot, Labour politician

An angry Parliamentary debate has the same effect upon national events as a slammed door has upon domestic arguments. It is emphatic; it is deeply, though momentarily, satisfying; and it settles nothing at all.
David Frost and Antony Jay, To England with Love, 1967

Westminster is the power house transmitting socially sanctioned aggression. It inevitably becomes the Mecca for all those who wish, even as they did in their nurseries, but now without fear of disapproval, to scream with anger, spit at their enemies, bitingly attack opponents, boldly hit out at wrongs, real and imagined. Like moths around a flame, the aggressive flutter around Westminster. Outside Dartmoor and the armed forces, there are no more aggressive men than those sitting in our Parliament.
Leo Abse, Private Member, 1973

The essentially feminine role of Parliament in the
constitutional process does indeed put one in mind
of the traditional wife in a male (or government)
dominated national household. What the master
says goes. Parliament may advise, complain,
criticise, protest, delay, nag, scream its head off
but it does what it likes in the end.
Norman Shrapnel, 1982

PROMISES

I am going to build the kind of nation that
President Roosevelt hoped for, President Truman
worked for and President Kennedy died for.
Lyndon B. Johnson, US Statesman 1964

He knows nothing and he thinks he knows
everything. That points clearly to a political career.
George Bernard Shaw, Major Barbara, 1905

PARTY POLITICS

A majority is always the best repartee.
Benjamin Disraeli, Tancred, Book 11

A conservative is a man with two perfectly good
legs who, however, has never learned to walk
forwards . . . A reactionary is a somnambulist
walking backwards . . . A radical is a man with
both feet firmly planted – in the air.
Franklin D. Roosevelt, Fireside Chat, 1939

When great questions end, little parties begin.
Walter Bagehot, English economist, critic

Party is the madness of many, for the gain of a
few.
Jonathan Swift

A sect or a party is an elegant incognito devised to
save a man from the vexation of thinking.
Ralph Waldo Emerson (1803-1882), American essayist,
poet, philosopher

The best party is but a kind of conspiracy against
the rest of the nation.
George Saville (1633-1695), Lord Halifax, English
statesman

Vote Labour and you build castles in the air.
Vote Conservative and you can live in them.
David Frost, television presenter, interviewer, *That Was
The Week That Was,* 1962

PATRIOTISM

My fellow Americans, ask not what your country
can do for you – ask what you can do for your
country.
John F. Kennedy

The summer soldier and the sunshine patriot will,
in this crisis, shrink from the service of their
country; but he that stands it NOW deserves the
love and thanks of man and woman.
Thomas Paine (1737-1809), revolutionary

Our country right or wrong. When right, to be
kept right; when wrong, to be put right.
Carl Schurz (1829-1906), German orator, later American
general and senator

We have got to be like the Irish – proud without
being silly, parochial without being worldly,
culturally secure without being culturally arrogant.
Paul Keating, Australian PM, in a speech to Irish-
Australian businessmen

PERSUASION

A political streetwalker accosting men with 'come
home with me, dear'.
Harold L. Ickes

P O L I C Y

The policy has become almost indistinguishable from the Tories with Kinnock performing more double somersaults than Major's father ever did in his chosen profession.
Arthur Scargill, 1992, of Labour leader Neil Kinnock

P O L I T I C A L   L I F E S T Y L E

The standard of Henry Clay should consist of his armorial bearings, which ought to be a pistol, a pack of cards, and a brandy bottle.
Anon

No one knew better than the Cock of Kentucky which side his bread was buttered on: and he liked butter. A considerable portion of his public life was spent in trying to find butter for both sides of the slice.
Irving Stone, of Henry Clay, *They Also Ran*

He reminds me of Henry VIII – not with all the doublet and hose, but at least well-fed.
Terry Dicks, of Tony Banks

Half the Tory Party is in love with Virginia Bottomley. Edwina Currie hopes the other half are in love with her.
Julian Critchley, 1993, of Virginia Bottomley, Health Minister

P O L I T I C I A N S

Politicians are people who, when they see light at the end of the tunnel, order more tunnel.
Sir John Quinton, chairman, Barclays Bank plc, 1989

The politician is an acrobat. He keeps his balance by saying the opposite of what he does.
Maurice Barres (1896-1923), *Mes cahiers*

98 per cent of the adults in this country are decent, hard-working, honest Americans. It's the other lousy two per cent that get all the publicity. But then – we elect them.
Lily Tomlin, comedienne

. . . a species of tetanus where one set of muscles goes rigid pulling against the another – and the patient becomes paralysed.
Sir Terence Beckett, then chairman of Ford Motor Company Ltd, on government interference in industry, 1978

Every politician is emphatically a promising politician.
G. K. Chesterton, The Red Moon of Meru

A politician will do anything to keep his job – even become a patriot.
William Randolph Hearst (1863-1951), editorial, 1933

A politician is a statesman who approaches every question with an open mouth.
Adlai Stevenson

A statesman is a politician who is held upright by equal pressure from all directions.
Eric A. Johnson (1896-1963), American entrepreneur

A politician thinks of the next election; a statesman, of the next generation.
James Freeman Clarke (1810-88), American theologian

Since a politician never believes what he says, he is surprised when others believe him.
Charles de Gaulle (attrib.)

When you're abroad you're a statesman: when you're at home you're just a politician.
Harold Macmillan, British statesman, 1958

Politicians are the same everywhere. They promise to build bridges even where there are no rivers.
Nikita Khrushchev, Soviet statesman (attrib.), 1960

Politicians are well meaning but they hold horizons of six months when, to run a business, you need a five-year view.
Sir William Barlow, chairman, BICC Plc, 1989

I've met Margaret Thatcher and, unfortunately, she has a trait of not being able to listen and a trait of being prepared to keep on talking.
Joe Gormley, then president, National Union of Mineworkers, 1980

It's like pressing your wife. If you press nice she will respond. But if you get up and say 'I'll knock your block off' she will hit you back.
Joe Gormley, on how to deal with Margaret Thatcher, 1981

No man is good enough to govern another man without the other's consent.
Abraham Lincoln, 1854

You can fool some of the people all the time and all the people some of the time; but you can't fool all the people all the time.
Abraham Lincoln

The proper memory for a politician is one that knows when to remember and when to forget.
John Morley (1838-1923), British statesman

He has never had a job. I tell you, if he applied to me for work I would not hire him.
Sir Gordon White, chairman of the board, Hanson Industries, on Neil Kinnock, 1990

The reason they think I'm bonkers is because I have original views and speak my mind.
Sir Nicholas Fairbairn, Conservative MP, 1993

If a minister just twists my arm I'll just stand there and have it twisted, but it'll be a long time before it falls off. Either you're a man who stands up for what he believes in or you're a chicken and fall apart.
Sir Denis Rooke, then chairman, British Gas plc, 1981

All politicians have vanity. Some wear it more gently than others.
David Steel, 1985

I used to say that politics was the second lowest profession and I have come to know that it bears a great similarity to the first.
Ronald Reagan

I hate all politicians. They're the biggest bunch of bums you can find.
Michael Caine

Nothing to see in their eyes. They all talk as though they're addressing a room filled with 40,000 people.
Robert Redford, 1974

The tragedy of one successful politician after another is the gradual substitution of narcissism for an interest in the community.
Bertrand Russell

Politicians are not people who seek power in order to implement policies they think necessary. They are people who seek policies in order to attain power.
Evelyn Waugh, author, critic

Our differences are politics, our agreements principles.
William McKinley (1843-1901), American Republican politician

Whenever a man has cast a longing eye on offices, a rottenness begins in his conduct.
Thomas Jefferson

A politician divides mankind into two classes: tools and enemies.
Friedrich Nietzsche

The first requirement of a statesman is that he be dull. This is not always easy to achieve.
Dean Acheson, American statesman, 1970

A horrible voice, bad breath and a vulgar manner – the characteristics of a popular politician.
Aristophanes

Politics should be the part-time profession of every citizen.
Dwight D. Eisenhower

Dangerous lunatics to be avoided when possible, and carefully humoured: people, above all, to whom we must never tell the truth.
W. H. Auden

Just to say the word 'politician' and I think of a chicanery.
Lucille Ball

The politicians owe their most valuable discovery to Phineas T. Barnum.
Columbia Record

P O L I T I C S

Politics is as a dog's life without a dog's decencies.
Rudyard Kipling

Politics, as the word is commonly understood, are nothing but corruptions.
Plato

Politics is perhaps the only profession for which no preparation is thought necessary.
Robert Louis Stevenson

Politics is the art of preventing people from busying themselves with what is their own business.
Paul Valéry (1871-1945), French poet and writer

A political convention is a chess tournament disguised as a circus.
Alistair Cooke

Political gas is not of the illuminating variety.
Columbia Record

Politics is the art of the next best.
Otto von Bismarck

I find politics the single most uninspiring, unemotional, insensitive activity on this planet.
Adam Ant, singer

He who gives food to the people will win.
Lech Walesa, Polish politician

When political ammunition runs low, inevitably the rusty artillery of abuse is always wheeled into action.
Adlai Stevenson, 1952

Practical politics consists in ignoring facts.
Henry B. Adams

I could not be leading a religious life unless I
identified myself with the whole of mankind, and
that I could not do unless I took part in politics.
M. K. Gandhi (1869-1948)

Politics is a blood sport.
Aneurin Bevan

Politics is the conduct of public affairs for private
advantage.
Otto von Bismarck

Politics are almost as exciting as war, and quite as
dangerous. In war you can only be killed once, but
in politics many times.
Sir Winston Churchill

Being in politics is like being a football coach. You
have to be smart enough to understand the game
and stupid enough to think it's important.
Eugene McCarthy

Politics is the art of looking for trouble, finding it
everywhere, diagnosing it incorrectly and applying
the wrong remedy.
Groucho Marx

The more you read about politics, the more you
get to admit that each party is worse than the
other.
Will Rogers

It is now known that men enter local politics
solely as a result of being unhappily married.
G. Northcote Parkinson, Parkinson's Law, 1957

All political questions, all matters of right, are at
bottom only questions of might.
August Bebel (1840-1913), German politician, 1871

Politics is a deleterious profession, like some
poisonous handicrafts. Men in power have no
opinions, but may be had cheap for any opinion
for any purpose.
Ralph Waldo Emerson, American writer, *The Conduct
of Life,* 1860

In politics, as in life or love, a lot depends on being in the right place at the right time. That's certainly what happened to me.
Senator Edward Kennedy, 1993

I have come to the conclusion that politics are too serious a matter to be left to the politicians.
Charles de Gaulle, French general and statesman (attrib.)

Politics makes estranged bedfellows.
Goodman Ace

The first requirement of a statesman is that he be dull. This is not always easy to achieve.
Dean Acheson, American statesman, 1970

A: Have you ever taken a serious political stand on anything?
B. Yes, for 24 hours I refused to eat grapes.
Woody Allen, Sleeper, 1973

There are three groups that no British Prime Minister should provoke: the Vatican, the Treasury and the miners.
Stanley Baldwin (attrib.)

In politics as on the sickbed people toss from one side to the other thinking they will be more comfortable.
Johann Goethe

I always wanted to get into politics but I was never light enough to get in the team.
Art Buchwald

If you take yourself seriously in politics, you've had it.
Lord Carrington, British Foreign Secretary

Political ability is the ability to foretell what is going to happen tomorrow, next week, next month and next year. And to have the ability afterward to explain why it didn't happen.
Winston Churchill

Politics is not the art of the possible. It consists in choosing between the disastrous and the unpalatable.
J. K. Galbraith, Ambassador's Journal, responding to R. A. Butler's *Politics is the Art of the Possible,* 1969

If American politics are too dirty for women to take part in, there's something wrong with American politics.
Edna Ferber (1887-1968), writer

I was not meant for the job or the spotlight of public life. Here ruining people is considered sport.
Vincent Foster, Clinton's aide in his suicide note

POVERTY

Poverty does not mean the possession of little, but the lack of much.
Antipater of Macedonia, c.397-c.319 BC, Macedonian general

So shall we break up the nation because of sausage?
Mikhail Gorbachev responding to Lithuanian complaints about shortages in the shops, 1990

Laws grind the poor, and rich men rule the law.
Oliver Goldsmith, (1728-74), Irish poet, playwright and novelist, *The Traveller,* 1765

This is not for me. The honour is for the poor.
Mother Teresa, on receiving the Order of Merit, 1983

To keep a lamp burning we have to keep putting oil in it.
Mother Teresa, 1975

POWER

When power narrows the areas of man's concern, poetry reminds him of the richness and diversity of its existence.
John F. Kennedy in his address at Dedication of the Robert Frost Library, 1963

Every Communist must grasp the truth: 'Political power grows out of the barrel of a gun.'
Mao Tse-Tung, Problems of War and Strategy, 1938

We give the impression of being in office but not in power.
Norman Lamont, Chancellor of the Exchequer, at the time of his resignation, describing how John Major is running the country, 1993

Men of power have not time to read; yet men who do not read are unfit for power.
Michael Foot, British politician and journalist, *Debts of Honour*

A friend in power is a friend lost.
Henry O. Adams, The Education of Henry Adams, 1906

Power corrupts, but lack of power corrupts absolutely.
Adlai Stevenson, 1963

Power is the ultimate aphrodisiac.
Henry Kissinger, quoted in the *Guardian,* 1976

It is certainly more agreeable to have power to give than to receive.
Sir Winston Churchill

There is only one right in the world and that right is one's own strength.
Adolf Hitler

Bureaucracy is a giant mechanism operated by pygmies.
Honoré de Balzac

Unlimited power is apt to corrupt the minds of those who possess it.
William Pitt the Elder, British statesman

If a woman like Eva Peron with no ideals can get that far, think how far I can go with all the ideals that I have.
Margaret Thatcher, 1980

U-turn if you want to. The lady's not for turning.
Margaret Thatcher, 1980

We have the power to make this the best
generation of mankind in the history of the world
– or to make it the last.
John F. Kennedy

We are the masters at the moment – and not only
for the moment, but for a very long time to come.
Lord Shawcross, British Labour politician and lawyer,
1946

If Nancy Reagan had been given a fraction of Mrs
Clinton's power the Democrats would have been in
uproar.
Senator Jesse Helms, Republican Party

If the person who has the last word at night is the
same person who has the first word in the
morning, they're going to be important. If they
also have an IQ of zillions and a backbone of steel,
it's a pretty safe assumption to say this is a person
of considerable influence.
James Carvile, Clinton's campaign strategist, summing
up Hillary Clinton's power, 1993

The reason we have been out of power for 15
years is simple – society changed and we refused to
change with it.
Tony Blair MP, 1994

PRAISE

The beauty of Scotland is that it is big enough to
be important in the UK and small enough for
everyone to know everyone else.
George Younger, Conservative politician, Secretary of
State for Scotland, 1982

PRESIDENCY

Mothers all want their sons to grow up to be
President but they don't want them to become
politicians in the process.
John F. Kennedy (attrib.)

If Presidents don't do it to their wives, they do it to the country.
Mel Brooks, American humorist

I'm not running for president, but if I did I'd win.
Donald Trump, American property developer, 1987

Politics means the art of compromise. Most politicians are all-too-well schooled in this art. They compromise to get nominated; they compromise to get elected; and they compromise time and time again, after they are elected, to stay in office.
Dick Gregory, *Why I Want to Be President*

The best reason I can think of for not running for President of the United States is that you have to shave twice a day.
Adlai Stevenson

All the President is, is a glorified public relations man who spends his time flattering, kissing, and kicking people to get them to do what they are supposed to do anyway.
Harry S. Truman, in a letter to his sister, 1947

I really don't think I'm worthy of the office, but I have to put the country before my own limitations.
Art Buchwald, American humorist

When I was a boy I was told that anybody could become President; I'm beginning to believe it.
Clarence Darrow (1857-1938), American lawyer, writer

Even the President of the United States sometimes must have to stand naked.
Bob Dylan

As President Nixon says, presidents can do almost anything, and President Nixon has done many things that nobody would have thought of doing.
Golda Meir, Israeli politician

Nothing would please the Kremlin more than to have the people of this country choose a second-rate President.
Richard Nixon

I feel very proud, even though they didn't elect me, to be President of the Argentines.
General Galatieri

In the Bob Hope Gold Classic the participation of President Gerald Ford was more than enough to remind you that the nuclear button was at one stage at the disposal of a man who might have either pressed it by mistake or else pressed it deliberately to obtain room service.
Clive James, Australian writer, critic

We're an ideal political family; as accessible as Disneyland.
Maureen Reagan, daughter of President Reagan

The buck stops here.
Harry S. Truman

How presidential is a man with a pussycat on his lap?
The Washington Post, referring to Bill Clinton's cat 'Socks'

I sit here all day trying to persuade people to do the thing they ought to have sense enough to do without my persuading them. That's all the powers of the President amount to.
Harry S. Truman

The President is weak. When a man is impotent, his girlfriend goes off with another man. In the same way the country now has to find a new president, a strong one.
Vladimir Zhirinovsky, leader, nationalist party, of Boris Yeltsin

I'm afraid he may have had it.
George Bush, on hearing of the coûp against Mikhail Gorbachev, 1991

I know Governor Thomas E. Dewey, and Mr Dewey is a fine man. Yes, Mr Dewey is a fine man. So is my Uncle Morris. My Uncle Morris shouldn't be President; neither should Dewey.
George Jessel

THE VICE-PRESIDENT

Once there were two brothers. One ran away to sea, the other was elected Vice-President, and nothing was ever heard of either of them again.
Thomas R. Marshall (1854-1925), American lawyer, Vice-President

PRESIDENTS OF THE USA

GEORGE BUSH (1988-92)
All hat and no cattle.
John Connally

Real men don't lob.
Runners World on his tennis style, 1988

JIMMY CARTER (1977-81)
Jimmy's basic problem is that he's super cautious.
He looks before and after he leaps.
Joey Adams, *New York Post,* 1978

We're realists. It doesn't make much difference
between Ford and Carter. Carter is your typical
smiling, brilliant, back-stabbing, bull-shitting
Southern nut-cutter.
Lane Kirkland, US trades union leader, 1976

I think Jimmy Carter as President is like Truman
Capote marrying Dolly Parton. The job is just too
big for him.
Rich Little (attrib.)

I would not want Jimmy Carter and his men put in
charge of snake control in Ireland.
Eugene McCarthy, 1976

Carter has done what no other President has done:
He has brought into the sharpest contrast the
hypocrisy of the US in respect to human rights.
Marlon Brando, actor

Carter is chicken-fried McGovern.
Robert Dole

If you're in the peanut business, you learn to think
small.
Eugene McCarthy

Jimmy Carter's running for WHAT?
Reg Murphy, *Atlanta Constitution,* 1974

Depression is when you are out of work. A
recession is when your neighbour is out of work.
A recovery is when Jimmy Carter is out of work.
Ronald Reagan

CALVIN COOLIDGE (1923-29)
. . . simply a cheap and trashy fellow, deficient in
sense and almost devoid of any notion of honour –
in brief, a dreadful little cad.
H. L. Mencken, 1924

He is the first president to discover that what the American people want is to be left alone.
Will Rogers, 1924

The greatest man who ever came out of Plymouth Corner, Vermont.
Clarence Darrow

BILL CLINTON (1993-)
President of the United States
I still believe in a place called Hope.
President-elect *Bill Clinton*

Don't tread on us.
Bill Clinton, warning Iraqi leader Saddam Hussein following the American missile attack on Baghdad in retaliation for an alleged plot to assassinate George Bush

Shorter than Kohl, taller than Major and younger than Jagger.
Today headline after Bill Clinton's election as president, 1992

The Prince of Sleaze
Jerry Brown, 1992

I have never seen . . . so slippery, so disgusting a candidate.
Nat Hentoff, Village Voice, 1992

An unmistakable fog of political incompetence is beginning to form around the White House.
The New York Times, on Bill Clinton

DWIGHT D. EISENHOWER (1953-61)
Eisenhower is the only living Unknown Soldier.
Robert S. Kerr, Oklahoma Senator

If I talk over people's heads, Ike must talk under their feet.
Adlai Stevenson, Democratic presidential candidate defeated by Eisenhower in 1952 and 1956

The General has dedicated himself so many times, he must feel like the cornerstone of a public building.
Adlai Stevenson

Meeting him was not at all like an experience in the modern world. More like meeting George III at Brighton.
Harold Macmillan

The trouble with Eisenhower is he's just a coward. He hasn't got any backbone at all.
Harry S. Truman

GERALD FORD (1974-77)
A year ago Gerald Ford was unknown throughout America. Now he's unknown throughout the world.
Anon., quoted in the *Guardian*, 1974

Richard Nixon impeached himself. He gave us Gerald Ford as his revenge.
Bella Abzug

Gerry Ford is a nice guy, but he played too much football with his helmet off.
Lyndon B. Johnson

If Ford can get away with this list of issues . . . and be elected on it, then I'm going to call the dictator of Uganda, Mr Amin, and tell him to start giving speeches on airport safety.
Walter Mondale

It troubles me that he played centre on the football team. That means he can only consider options for the twenty yard in either direction and that he has spent a good deal of his life looking at the world upside down through his legs.
Martin Peretz, Editorial Director, *New Republic*

He's alive but unconscious, just like Gerald Ford.
Airplane, 1980

Gerald Ford is the first President of the United States to be elected by a majority of one – and nobody demanded a recount.
Laurence J. Peter

Gerry Ford is so dumb that he can't fart and chew gum at the same time.
Lyndon B. Johnson, US statesman, quoted in
A Ford not a Lincoln

ULYSSES SIMPSON GRANT (1869-71)

No terms except unconditional and immediate surrender can be accepted. I propose to move immediately upon your works.
Ulysses Grant, message to opposing commander, Simon Bolivar Buckner, during siege of Fort Donelson, 1862

I propose to fight it out on this line, if it takes all summer.
Ulysses Grant, in a dispatch to Washington, 1864

Let us have peace.
Ulysses Grant, on accepting Presidential nomination, 1868

I know no method to secure the repeal of bad or obnoxious laws so effective as their stringent execution.
Ulysses Grant, Inaugural address, 1869

The people are tired of a man who has not an idea above a horse or a cigar.
Joseph Brown, 1871

How is it that Grant, who was behind at Fort Henry, drunk at Donelson, surprised at Shiloh and driven back from Oxford, Miss., is still in command?
Murat Halstead, 1863

WARREN G. HARDING (1921-23)

His speeches left the impression of an army of pompous phrases moving over the landscape in search of an idea; sometimes these meandering words would actually capture a straggling thought and bear it triumphantly a prisoner in their midst, until it died of servitude and overwork.
William G. McAdoo, unsuccessful contender for Democratic nomination for president, 1920 and 1924

HERBERT HOOVER (1929-33)

I was just standing out in front watching the other acts when a lady walked up to me in the lobby and said, 'Pardon me, young man, could you tell me where I could find the rest room?' and I said, 'It's just around the corner.' 'Don't give me that Hoover talk,' she said. 'I'm serious.'
Al Boasbert, for Bob Hope, 1930

LYNDON B. JOHNSON (1963-69)

After two weeks in office – the editors of *National Review* regretfully announce that their patience with President Lyndon B. Johnson is exhausted.
William Buckley Jr, *The National Review,* 1965

He fiddled while Rome burned and faddled while men died.
Barry Goldwater

JOHN F. KENNEDY (1961-63)

We stand today on the edge of a new frontier.
John F. Kennedy, on his nomination as Presidential candidate, Democratic Party Convention, 1960

In free society art is not a weapon . . . Artists are not engineers of the soul.
John F. Kennedy, address at Dedication of the Robert Frost Library, 1963

When we got into office, the one thing that surprised me most was to find that things were just as bad as we'd been saying they were.
John F. Kennedy, at his birthday party at the White House, 1961

We must use time as a tool, not as a couch.
John F. Kennedy, 1961

. . . the report is that Old Joe Kennedy told Young Jack: 'Don't worry, son, if you lose the election, I'll buy you a country.'
Time, 1960

His speaking style is pseudo-Roman: 'Ask not what your country can do for you . . .'
Why not say, 'Don't ask . . .'?
'Ask not . . .' is the style of a man playing the role of being President, not of a man being President.
Herb Gold, of J. F. Kennedy, *New York Post,* 1962

Everyone's talking about how young the candidates are. And it's true. A few months ago Kennedy's mother said, 'You have a choice . . . do you want to go to camp this year, or run for President?'
Bob Hope, during the Kennedy/Nixon presidential campaign, 1960

Do you realise the responsibility I carry? I'm the only person standing between Nixon and the White House.
John F. Kennedy, to Arthur Schlesinger (Richard Nixon was the Republican candidate in the 1960 US Presidential Election)

Kennedy after all has lots of glamour – Gregory Peck with an atom bomb in his holster.
William F. Buckley, Jr, *The National Review,* 1963

The enviably attractive nephew who sings an Irish ballad for the company and then winsomely disappears before the table clearing and dishwashing begin.
Lyndon B. Johnson

It is said the President is willing to laugh at himself. That is fine. But when is he going to extend that privilege to us?
Mort Sahl

ABRAHAM LINCOLN (1860-65)
Abe – have you got a pencil and paper there? Would you take this down? 'You can fool all of the people some of the time and some of the people all of the time. But you can't fool all of the people all the time.' . . . Well, you keep doing it differently, Abe. The last quote I got was 'You can fool all the people all the time . . .'
Bob Newhart, *Abe Lincoln versus Madison Avenue,* 1960

This man's appearance, his pedigree, his coarse low jokes and anecdotes, his vulgar similes and his frivolity, are a disgrace to the seat he holds.
John Wilkes Booth

He is a Barbarian, Scythian, Yahoo, a gorilla in respect of outward polish, but a most sensible, straightforward old codger.
George T. Strong

RICHARD NIXON (1969-74)

Richard M. Nixon in Washington, so the story goes, Republican top strategists huddled, and all were glum indeed – except one. 'I'm sure we'll win, there's no doubt about it,' he enthused. Everyone wanted to know the reason for his confidence. Answer: 'I have a deep and abiding faith in the fundamental bigotry of the American people.'
Time, the Republican Presidential candidate was Nixon, 1960

Look, Nixon's no dope. If the people really *wanted* moral leadership, he'd give them moral leadership.
Charles Barsotti, cartoon in the *New Yorker*

Nixon just isn't half the man Hitler was.
Richard Dudman, St Louis Post Dispatch

Ever since Nixon, nobody has asked me why I am teaching a course like Policy Choice as Value Conflict.
Professor Bruce Payne, Duke University, North Carolina

Richard Nixon means never having to say you're sorry.
Wilfrid Sheed, GQ, 1984

He is the kind of politician who would cut down a redwood tree and then mount the stump to make a speech for conservation.
Adlai Stevenson, 1956

Richard Nixon is a no-good lying bastard. He can lie out of both sides of his mouth at the same time, and even if he caught himself telling the truth, he'd lie just to keep his hand in.
Harry S. Truman

. . . it is quite extraordinary! He will even tell a lie when it is not convenient to. That is the sign of a great artist.
Gore Vidal, 1972

. . . there is no petting . . . Modern couples just strip their clothes off and go at it . . . blame must . . . be placed on ex-President Nixon's decision to let the US dollar float in relation to other Western currencies. More than a decade of monetary instability has conditioned people to utilise their assets immediately. If the sex urge is not spent forthwith, it might degenerate into something less valuable – affection, for instance.
P. J. O'Rourke, Modern Manners, 1983

In all my years of public life I have never obstructed justice . . . Your President is no crook!
Richard M. Nixon

I let down my friends, I let down my country. I let down our system of government.
Richard Nixon, 1973

Dick Nixon – before he dicks you.
Bumper sticker, 1973

I wouldn't trust Nixon from here to that phone.
Barry Goldwater, Newsweek, 1986

Avoid all needle drugs – the only dope worth shooting is Richard Nixon.
Abbie Hoffman, 1971

Our founders did not oust George II in order for us to crown Richard I.
Ralph Nader, 1975

He forever perplexes and annoys. Every time you think he is about to show the statesmanship for which his intelligence and experience have equipped him, he throws a spitball.
Ronald Steel, 1985

Last Thursday Mr Nixon dismissed me as 'another Truman'. I regard this as a compliment. I consider him another Dewey.
John F. Kennedy

RONALD REAGAN (1981-88)

He has not the remotest idea of what he is about
to say, and having said it he has not the remotest
recollection of what it was. One can pray only that
the Russians are alive to this fact, since if they are
not, then none of us will be alive to anything else.
Alan Coren, Punch, 1984

I believe that Ronald Reagan can make this
country what it once was – an arctic region
covered with ice.
Steven Martin, American actor (attrib.)

. . . a triumph of the embalmer's art.
Gore Vidal, 1981

I still think Nancy does most of his talking; you'll
notice that she never drinks water when Ronnie
speaks.
Robin Williams, US actor, 1982

Reaganomics, that makes sense to me. It means if
you don't have enough money, it's because poor
people are hoarding it.
Kevin Rooney, GQ, 1984

Politics is not a bad profession. If you succeed
there are many rewards, if you disgrace yourself
you can always write a book.
Ronald Reagan

Ronald Reagan has violated every principle for
which America stands. He denies the jurisdiction
of the World Court; he acts without consulting
Congress and in opposition to the advice of US
allies. Serving as judge, jury and executioner, he
orders military strikes that kill civilians . . . The
President has no legal power to order US forces to
murder indiscriminately and to terrorise those he
styles his enemies. Such acts constitute high crimes
and misdemeanours. Reagan's subversion of the
principles of truth and the rule of law is the
greatest threat facing the American people and the
world.
Ramsay Clark, former US Attorney-General

I've always believed there is a certain divine scheme of things. I'm not quite able to explain how my election happened or why I'm here, apart from believing it is part of God's plan for me.
Ronald Reagan, on attaining governorship of California, 1966

No one can kill Americans and brag about it. No one.
Ronald Reagan, 1986

You know, by the time you reach my age, you've made plenty of mistakes if you've lived your life properly.
Ronald Reagan, 1987

They say hard work never hurt anybody, but I figure why take the chance.
Ronald Reagan (attrib.)

A true velvet fascist.
Shirley MacLaine, actress

That youthful sparkle in his eye is caused by his contact lenses, which he keeps highly polished.
Sheila Graham, The Times

In the heat of a political lifetime, Reagan innocently squirrels away titbits of misinformation and then, sometimes years later, casually drops them into his public discourse, like gumballs in a quiche.
Lucy Howard, Newsweek, 1985

I listen to Reagan and I want to throw up.
Henry Fonda, actor, 1981

Q. What do you get if you cross James Dean with Ronald Reagan?
A. A rebel without a clue.
Q. How many Reagan cabinet ministers does it take to change a lightbulb?
A. None – they prefer to keep Ron in the dark!
Playboy, 1988

What's really worrying about Reagan is that he always seems to be waiting for someone to say 'Cut' and has no idea how they've decided the script should end.
Katherine Whitehorn, The Observer, 1983

Reagan is slightly to the right of the Sheriff of
Nottingham.
Johnny Carson

Washington could not tell a lie; Nixon could not
tell the truth; Reagan cannot tell the difference.
Mort Sahl

You don't have to be smart to act – look at the
outgoing President of the United States.
Cher, Playboy, 1988

FRANKLIN D. ROOSEVELT (1933-45)
. . . the man started more creations than were ever
begun since Genesis – and finished none.
Hugh Johnson, Director, National Recovery
Administration

If he became convinced tomorrow that coming out
for cannibalism would get him the votes he so
sorely needs, he would begin fattening a
missionary in the White House backyard come
Wednesday . . .
H. L. Mencken (attrib.)

A bull-headed man whose high place in the 'New
Deal' was won by his ability to waste more money
in quicker time on more absurd undertakings than
any other mischievous twit in Washington could
think of.
Chicago Tribune, of Harry Hopkins, Adviser to
F. D. Roosevelt

Stalin hates the guts of all your top people. He
thinks he likes me better, and I hope he will
continue to do so.
Franklin D. Roosevelt, The Hinge of Fate

A chameleon on plaid.
Herbert Hoover

Two-thirds mush and one-third Eleanor.
Alice Roosevelt-Longworth

Thomas Jefferson founded the Democratic Party;
Franklin Roosevelt dumbfounded it.
Dewey Short

THEODORE ROOSEVELT (1901-9)

One always thinks of him as a glorified bouncer engaged eternally in cleaning out bar-rooms – and not too proud to gouge when the inspiration came to him or to bite in the clinches.
H. L. Mencken, Prejudices, Second Series, 1920

The great virtue of my radicalism lies in the fact that I am perfectly ready, if necessary, to be radical on the conservation side.
Theodore Roosevelt, 1906

My father always wanted to be the corpse at every funeral, the bride at every wedding and the baby at every christening.
Alice Roosevelt-Longworth, of Theodore Roosevelt

HARRY S. TRUMAN (1945-53)

Any man who has had the job I've had and didn't have a sense of humour wouldn't still be here.
Harry S. Truman, 1955 (attrib.)

To err is Truman.
Republican Party slogan, 1948

My choice early in life was either to be piano-player in a whorehouse or a politician. And to tell the truth, there's hardly any difference.
Harry S. Truman, 1962

Truman . . . seemed to stand for nothing more spectacular than honesty in war contracting, which was like standing for virtue in Hollywood or adequate rainfall in the Middle West.
George E. Allen, Presidents Who Have Known Me

GEORGE WASHINGTON, First US President (1789-97)

That Washington was not a scholar is certain. That he is too illiterate, unlearned, unread for his station and reputation is equally beyond dispute.
John Adams, 1782

WOODROW WILSON (1913-21)

Mr Wilson's name among the Allies is like that of the rich uncle, and they have accepted his manners out of respect for his means.
Morning Post, 1919

Mr Wilson's mind, as has been the custom, will be closed all day Sunday.
George S. Kaufman

The spacious philanthropy which he exhaled upon Europe stopped quite sharply at the coasts of his own country.
Sir Winston Churchill, The World Crisis, 1929

The French will only be united under the threat of danger. Nobody can simply bring together a country that has 265 kinds of cheese.
Charles de Gaulle, 1951

Mr Wilson bores me with his 'Fourteen Points'; why God Almighty has only ten.
George Clemenceau

I am suspicious of a man who has a handshake like a ten-cent pickled mackerel in brown paper.
William A. White

PRIME MINISTERS

Above any other position of eminence, that of Prime Minister is filled by fluke.
Enoch Powell, 1987

CLEMENT ATTLEE (1945-51)
He seems determined to make a trumpet sound like a tin whistle . . . he brings to the fierce struggle of politics that tepid enthusiasm of a lazy summer afternoon at a cricket match.
Aneurin Bevan, 1945

Absolutely true – but then he [Clement Attlee] does have a lot to be modest about.
Sir Winston Churchill, agreeing with a colleague that Attlee was modest.

. . . reminds me of nothing so much as a dead fish before it has had time to stiffen.
George Orwell, writer (attrib.)

Charisma? He did not recognise the word except as a clause in his beloved *Times* crossword.
James Margach, The Abuse of Power, 1981

He is a modest little man with much to be modest about.
Sir Winston Churchill, of Clement Attlee

STANLEY BALDWIN (1923-24, 1924-29, 1935-37)
He occasionally stumbled over the truth, but hastily picked himself up and hurried on as if nothing had happened.
Sir Winston Churchill (attrib.)

I think Baldwin has gone mad. He simply takes one jump in the dark; looks round; and then takes another.
Lord Birkenhead, letter to Austen Chamberlain, 1923

One could not even dignify him with the name of stuffed shirt. He was simply a hole in the air.
George Orwell, The Lion and the Unicorn, 1941

ANEURIN (NYE) BEVAN (1945-51)
I have never regarded politics as the arena of morals. It is the arena of interests.
Aneurin Bevan

If thy Nye offend thee, pluck it out.
Clement Attlee, speech to the Labour NEC, 1955

He will be as great a curse to this country in peace as he was a squalid nuisance in time of war.
Sir Winston Churchill, 1945

Such a gift horse to his opponents that it would be ungrateful for us to look him in the mouth.
Violet Bonham-Carter (Lady Asquith) (1887-1969),
British Liberal politician, of Nye Bevan

ANDREW BONAR-LAW (1858-1923)
Has not the brains of a Glasgow baillie.
Herbert Asquith, 1916

Bonar would never make up his mind on anything. Once a question had been decided, Bonar would stick to it and fight for it to a finish, but he would never help in the taking of a decision.
David Lloyd-George

JAMES CALLAGHAN (1976-79)
Living proof that the short-term schemer and the frustrated bully can be made manifest in one man.
Hugo Young, Sunday Times, 1980

NEVILLE CHAMBERLAIN (1937-40)

Listening to a speech by Chamberlain is like paying a visit to Woolworth's. Everything in its place and nothing above sixpence.
Aneurin Bevan, House of Commons, 1937

. . . the mind and manner of a clothes-brush.
Harold Nicolson, critic, 1938

He has the lucidity which is the by-product of a fundamentally sterile mind.
Aneurin Bevan, British Labour politician

WINSTON CHURCHILL (1940-45, 1951-55)

I thought he was a young man of promise; but it appears he was a young man of promises.
A. J. Balfour of Winston Churchill, 1899

He refers to a defeat as a disaster as though it came from God, but to a victory as though it came from himself.
Aneurin Bevan, 1942

Churchill was fundamentally what the English call unstable – by which they mean anybody who has that touch of genius which is inconvenient in normal times.
Harold Macmillan, 1975

Comparing him to a cake – one layer was certainly 17th century. The 18th century in him is obvious. There was the 19th century, and a large slice, of course, of the 20th century: and another, curious, layer, which may possibly have been the 21st.
Clement Attlee

World Crisis – Winston has written four volumes about himself and called it *World Crisis.*
Arthur Balfour, 1899

The mediocrity of his thinking is concealed by the majesty of his language.
Aneurin Bevan

He is not a man for whom I ever had esteem. Always in the wrong, always surrounded by crooks, a most unsuccessful father – simply a 'Radio personality' who outlived his prime.
Evelyn Waugh, 1965

BENJAMIN DISRAELI (1868, 1874-76)
Every man has a right to be conceited until he is
successful.
Benjamin Disraeli

DAVID LLOYD GEORGE (1916-22)
He couldn't see a belt without hitting below it.
Margot Asquith, in her autobiography, 1936

He spent his whole life in plastering together the
true and the false and there from extracting the
plausible.
Stanley Baldwin

He did not seem to care which way he travelled,
providing he was in the driver's seat.
*Lord Beaverbrook, The Decline and Fall of Lloyd
George,* 1963

The Happy Warrior of Squandermania.
Sir Winston Churchill, debate in House of Commons
on 1929 Budget

Trying to argue with Lloyd George is like trying to
go for a walk with a grasshopper.
Eamonn de Valera

Lloyd George is rooted in nothing. He is void and
without content.
John M. Keynes, Essays

This goat-footed bard, this half-human visitor of
our age from the bag-ridden magic and enchanted
woods of Celtic antiquity.
John M. Keynes, Essays

If only I could piss the way he talks.
George Clemenceau

Not as nice as he looks.
Sir Winston Churchill

WILLIAM EWART GLADSTONE (1868-74,
1800-85, 1886, 1892-94)
. . . honest in the most odious sense of the word.
Benjamin Disraeli (attrib.)

They told me how Mr Gladstone read Homer for
fun, which I thought served him right.
Sir Winston Churchill, My Early Life, 1930

Mr Gladstone speaks to me as if I were a public meeting.
Queen Victoria (attrib.)

A sophistical rhetorician, inebriated with the exuberance of his own verbosity.
Benjamin Disraeli

I do not object to Gladstone's always having the ace of trumps up his sleeve, but only to his pretence that God had put it there.
Henry Labouchere (1831-1912), English journalist, politician

EDWARD HEATH (1970-74)
In any civilised country Heath would have been left hanging upside-down on a petrol pump years ago.
Auberon Waugh, *Private Eye,* 1974

'Travels' – A reminder that *Morning Cloud*'s skipper is no stranger to platitude and longitude.
Christopher Wordsworth, quoted in *The Observer*

It is the unpleasant and unacceptable face of capitalism but one should not suggest that the whole of the British industry consists of practices of this kind.
Edward Heath, referring to the Lonrho Affair, May 1973

SIR ALEC DOUGLAS-HOME (1963-64)
There are two problems in my life. The political ones are insoluble and the economic ones are incomprehensible.
Sir Alec Douglas-Home

JAMES RAMSAY MacDONALD (1924, 1929-31, 1931-35)
I have waited fifty years to see the Boneless Wonder sitting on the Treasury bench.
Sir Winston Churchill, House of Commons, 1933

We know that he has, more than any other man, the gift of compressing the largest amount of words into the smallest amount of thought.
Sir Winston Churchill, 1933

He has sufficient conscience to bother him, but not sufficient to keep him straight.
David Lloyd George

HAROLD MACMILLAN, Lord Stockton (1957-63)
The Prime Minister has an absolute genius for putting flamboyant labels on empty luggage.
Aneurin Bevan, of Harold Macmillan

Greater love hath no man than this, that he lay down his friends for his life.
Jeremy Thorpe, British Liberal politician, remark following a Cabinet reorganisation by Prime Minister Harold Macmillan

It was almost impossible to believe that he was anything but a down-at-heel actor resting between engagements at the decrepit theatres of minor provincial towns.
Bernard Levin, The Pendulum Years, 1976

The Right Honourable Gentleman has inherited the streak of charlatanry in Disraeli without his vision and the self-righteousness of Gladstone without his dedication to principle.
Harold Wilson

JOHN MAJOR (1990-)
I am fit, I am well, and I am here – and I'm staying.
John Major, hitting back at his critics, hours after the polls gave the lowest ever popularity rating for a Premier, 1993

We have a Prime Minister who avoids reality by pretending that it can be washed away in a mug of warm beer.
Bryan Gould, Labour MP

He has the precise opposite of the Midas Touch – from Black Wednesday to the pits closure fiasco, to mysteries of whatever the Government's new economic policy is, his baleful presence courts disaster.
Labour leader *John Smith* on Prime Minister John Major

No so much a wet, but a wimp.
Denis Healey, 1992

He acted less like a Prime Minister than a little
boy caught out fibbing at school.
The Daily Mirror, 1992

Poor John Major. What can you say except he will
always look grey like his Spitting Image puppet.
Peter Howarth, GQ, 1992

I do not accept the idea that all of a sudden Major
is his own man . . . There isn't such a thing as
Majorism.
Margaret Thatcher, 1992

HENRY PALMERSTON (1855-58, 1859-65)
Your Lordship is like a favourite footman on easy
terms with his mistress. Your dexterity seems a
happy compound of the smartness of an attorney's
clerk and the intrigue of a Greek lower empire.
Benjamin Disraeli

SIR ROBERT PEEL (1788-1850)
His smile is like the silver plate on a coffin.
Daniel O'Connell, quoting J.P. Curran, *Hansard,* 1835

His life has been one great appropriation clause. A
burglar of others' intellect – there is no statesman
who has committed political larceny on so grand a
scale.
Benjamin Disraeli

The Right Honourable Gentleman is reminiscent
of a poker. The only difference is that a poker
gives off occasional signs of warmth.
Benjamin Disraeli

I have no small talk and Peel has no manners.
Duke of Wellington

SPENCER PERCEVAL (1809-12)
It is a great misfortune to Mr Perceval to write in
a style that would disgrace a washerwoman.
King George IV, 1812

Mr Perceval is a very little man.
Lord Sidmouth, 1809

WILLIAM PITT the Younger (1783-1800, 1803-6)
He was not merely a chip off the old block, but
the old block itself.
Edmund Burke

The great snorting bawler.
William Cobber, *Rural Rides*

Pitt deem'd himself an Eagle – what a flat!
What was he? A poor wheeling, fluttering Bat –
An Imp of Darkness – busy catching flies!
Here, there, up, down, off, on – shriek, shriek –
snap, snap -
His gaping mouth a very lucky trap.
Quick seizing for his hungry maw – Supplies.
John Wolcott, *Odes to the Ins and Outs*

MARQUIS OF ROCKINGHAM (1765-66, 1782)
He could neither speak nor write with ease, and
was handicapped by inexperience, boils, and a
passion for Newmarket.
O. A. Sherard

LORD ROSEBERY (1894-95)
He is a one-eyed man in blinkers.
David Lloyd George

A man who never misses an occasion to let slip an
opportunity.
G. B. Shaw

A dark horse in a loose box.
John Morley

LORD JOHN RUSSELL (1846-52, 1865)
He was impulsive, very selfish, vain, and often
reckless and impulsive.
Queen Victoria, in her diary, 1878

If a traveller were informed that such a man was
the Leader of the House of Commons, he might
begin to comprehend how the Egyptians
worshipped an insect.
Benjamin Disraeli

The foreign policy of the Noble Earl . . . may be
summed up in two truly expressive words,
'meddle' and 'muddle'.
Lord Derby, 1864

ROBERT CECIL, LORD SALISBURY (1885-1902)
That strange, powerful, inscrutable and brilliant
obstructive deadweight at the top.
Lord George Curzon

I am always very glad when Lord Salisbury makes a great speech. It is sure to contain at least one blazing indiscretion which it is a delight to remember.
A. E. Parker, 1887

His face is livid, gaunt his white body, his breath green with gall, his tongue drips poison.
John Quincey Adams

MARGARET THATCHER (1979-90)
No woman in my time will be Prime Minister or Chancellor or Foreign Secretary – not the top jobs. Anyway I wouldn't want to be Prime Minister. You have to give yourself 100 per cent.
Margaret Thatcher, 1969

I was thinking as I was writing this book, about when Margaret Thatcher lost her virginity . . . or indeed if she ever did.
Baroness Barbara Castle, promoting her memoirs to the ladies of Chichester, 1993

I am a great admirer of Mrs Thatcher. She's one of the most splendid headmistresses there has ever been.
Arthur Marshall, Any Questions, 1982

. . . She is democratic enough to talk down to anyone.
Austin Mitchell, Westminster Man, 1982

Margaret Thatcher will never speak well on the television. Her impulse to tell the microphone to pull itself together is too great.
Edward Pearce, The Senate of Lilliput, 1983

She is trying to wear the trousers of Winston Churchill.
Leonid Brezhnev, 1979

She cannot see an institution without hitting it with her handbag.
Julian Critchley, The Times, 1982

She is a cross between Isadora Duncan and Lawrence of Arabia.
Daily Telegraph, 1986

The improbable PM; she seems totally humourless, with the nervous system usually attributed to fishes. Surely she has never read a book or looked at a picture?
Ann Fleming, 1985

Attila the Hen.
Clement Freud, 1979

If I were married to her, I'd be sure to have dinner ready when she got home.
George Shultz, American Secretary of State (attrib.)

There comes a time in every man's life when he must make way for an older man.
Reginald Maudling, on being dropped from Mrs Thatcher's Shadow Cabinet, 1976

She's the best man in England.
Ronald Reagan

This woman is headstrong, obstinate and dangerously self-opinionated.
Report by Personnel Officer at ICI rejecting her for a job in 1948

I'll stay until I'm tired of it. So long as Britain needs me, I shall never be tired of it.
Margaret Thatcher

The nanny seemed to be extinct until 1975, when, like the coelacanth, she suddenly and unexpectedly reappeared in the shape of Margaret Thatcher.
Simon Hoggart, Vanity Fair, 1983

She is the Enid Blyton of economics. Nothing must be allowed to spoil her simple plots.
Richard Holme, 1980

I hope Mrs Thatcher will go until the turn of the century looking like Queen Victoria.
Norman Tebbit, 1987

It was then that the iron entered my soul.
Margaret Thatcher, on her time in Edward Heath's Cabinet

She has fought resolutely for the class she represents and there are some lessons we might learn from that.
Tony Benn, British Labour politician

She approaches the problem of our country with all the one-dimensional subtlety of a comic strip.
Denis Healey, 1979

For the past few months she has been charging about like a bargain basement Boadicea.
Denis Healey, 1982

La Pasionara of middle-age privilege.
Denis Healey, 1986

I love being the centre of things.
Margaret Thatcher, 1984

I wasn't lucky, I deserved it.
Margaret Thatcher, after receiving a school prize, aged nine

Oh, I have got lots of human weaknesses, who hasn't?
Margaret Thatcher, The Times, 1983

I don't mind how much my ministers talk – as long as they do what I say.
Margaret Thatcher, The Times, 1987

I cannot bring myself to vote for a woman who has been voice-trained to speak to me as though my dog has just died.
Keith Waterhouse

Margaret Thatcher's great strength seems to be the better people know her, the better they like her. But, of course, she has one great disadvantage – she is a daughter of the people and looks trim, as the daughters of the people desire to be. Shirley Williams has such an advantage over her because she's a member of the upper-middle class and can achieve that kitchen-sink-revolutionary look that one cannot get unless one has been to a really good school.
Rebecca West (Cicely Isabel Fairfield) (1892-1983), British novelist, journalist, 1976

The lady may never have been for turning but she certainly turned heads. Everybody flirted with the Prime Minister. I think she took it as her due that you should flirt with her.
Alan Clark, former Defence Secretary, 1993

An ex-spam hoarder from Grantham presiding over the social and economic decline of our country.
Tony Banks

Mrs Thatcher is a very tough lady – you could bounce golf balls off her and she wouldn't notice.
Sir Rhodes Boyson, 1990

She behaves like a superannuated Sumo-wrestler.
Denis Healey

She adds the diplomacy of Alf Garnett to the economics of Arthur Daley.
Denis Healey

She has the mouth of Marilyn Monroe, and the eyes of Caligula.
François Mitterrand

SIR ROBERT WALPOLE (1721-42)
Achieving of nothing – still promising wonders –
By dint of experience improving in blunders,
Oppressing true merit, exalting the base,
And selling his country to purchase his place.
A jobber of stocks by retailing false news –
A prater at court in the style of the stews:
Of virtue and worth by profession a giber,
Of injuries and senates the bully and briber.
Though I name not the wretch, yet you know whom I mean –
'Tis the cur-dog of Britain, and spaniel of Spain.
Jonathan Swift, of Sir Robert Walpole

HAROLD WILSON (1964-1970, 1974-1976)
The only reason Harold Wilson as a child had to go to school without boots on, was that his boots were probably too small for him.
Harold Macmillan (attrib.)

Talk about a credibility gap, Harold Wilson is undoubtedly the world's most unbelievable politician. Indeed, one could have made a handsome living over the past three years betting on the opposite of everything Harold Wilson has averred, whether on Rhodesia, the common market, economic controls, or – most recently – the value of the pound.
William F. Buckley Jr, *On the Right,* 1967

The Rt Hon. Gentleman always keeps his ear so close to the ground that I suppose he is bound to get it full of dirt.
Sir Jocelyn Simon

All facts and no bloody ideas.
Aneurin Bevan

He's a waste-paper basket, filled with lightly given promises and pledges.
Iain MacLeod

When it comes to naked party politics, no Prime Minister has ever made such an idiot of himself by flagrantly broken promises as Mr Harold Wilson.
Sir Gerald Nabarro

George Brown drunk is a better man than the Prime Minister sober.
The Times

John F. Kennedy has described himself as an idealist without illusions. Harold Wilson is an illusionist without ideals.
Iain MacLeod

PROFIT

Without competition the pursuit of profit is immoral and mere exploitation.
Sir Keith Joseph, former Secretary of State for Industry, 1978

One of the important things this government has tried to do is rehabilitate the idea of profit in political discourse. I don't think the man in the street ever thought that profit was a dirty word, but it had almost become a dirty word among the intelligentsia.
Nigel Lawson, then Chancellor of the Exchequer, 1976

PROTEST

One fifth of the people are against everything all the time.
Robert Kennedy

Yippies, hippies, yahoos, Black Panthers, lions and tigers alike – I'd swap the whole damn zoo for the kind of young Americans I saw in Vietnam.
Spiro Agnew, American Republican politician

If any demonstrator ever lays down in front of my car, it'll be the last car he'll ever lay down in front of.
George C. Wallace, American Independent politician

PUBLICITY

Public relations is organised lying.
Lord Wilson, former Labour Prime Minister

QUOTATIONS

The wisdom of the wise and the experience of the ages are perpetuated by quotations.
Benjamin Disraeli

It is a good thing for an uneducated man to read books of quotations.
Sir Winston Churchill

You've got to be careful quoting Ronald Reagan, because when you quote him accurately it's called mud-slinging.
Walter F. Mondale, American Democratic politician

RACISM

Segregation now, segregation tomorrow and
segregation forever!
George C. Wallace, American Independent politician

I don't think you'll have to worry that this mental
midget, this hillbilly Hitler from Alabama, is
anywhere near becoming the nominee of the
Democratic Party.
Julian Bond, Black activist of George Wallace, Governor
of Alabama and Independent and Presidential Candidate,
1968

It's high time the rednecks came back to
Washington. There are a hell of a lot more
rednecks out there than people who eat crêpes
suzette.
Mickey Griffin, campaign organiser for George Wallace

Segregation is the adultery of an illicit intercourse
between injustice and immorality.
Martin Luther King, civil rights leader

No one has been barred on account of his race
from fighting or dying for America – there are no
'white' or 'coloured' signs on the foxholes or
graveyards of battle.
John F. Kennedy

I have no purpose to introduce political and social
equality between the white and black races. There
is a physical difference between the two, which, in
my judgment, will probably for ever forbid their
living together upon the footing of perfect
equality; and inasmuch as it becomes a necessity
that there must be a difference, . . . I am in favour
of the race to which I belong having the superior
position.
Abraham Lincoln

I tremble for my country when I reflect that God is
just; that his justice cannot sleep forever.
Thomas Jefferson

The truth is that Mozart, Pascal, Boolean algebra, Shakespeare, parliamentary government, baroque churches, Newton, the emancipation of women, Kant, Marx, and Ballanchine ballets don't redeem what this particular civilisation has wrought upon the world. The white race is the cancer of human history.
Susan Sontag, American essayist

Slavery is founded on the selfishness of man's nature – opposition to it on his love of justice. These principles are in eternal antagonism; and when brought into collision so fiercely as slavery extension brings them, shocks and throes and convulsions must ceaselessly follow.
Abraham Lincoln

In all social systems there must be a class to do the mean duties . . . It constitutes the very mudsills of society . . . Fortunately for the South, she found a race adapted to that purpose . . . We use them for that purpose and call them slaves.
J. H. Hammond (1807-1864), American senator, 1858

It seems that the British Government sees black people as expendable.
Bishop Desmond Tutu, Archbishop of Johannesburg and campaigner against apartheid, 1986

Until justice is blind to colour, until education is unaware of race, until opportunity is unconcerned with the colour of men's skins, emancipation will be a proclamation but not a fact.
Lyndon B. Johnson

The Americans ought to be ashamed of themselves for letting their medals be won by Negroes.
Adolf Hitler

They wear white sheets and their hats have a point – which is more than can be said for their beliefs.
David Frost, 1986, on the Ku Klux Klan

The Ku Klux Klan has been the vulture of America for almost a century. It is one enemy that has engaged in continual warfare against America since the Civil War. It's all hatred. Its weapon is fear. The Klan runs like a bloody thread through the noose every subversive outfit was eager to wrap around America's neck.
Walter Winchell

There are too many toss-pots in the Cabinet already. He should have been a candidate in Wolverhampton, where his colour would have been more appropriate.
Dudley Aldridge, former Mayor of Cheltenham, of John Taylor, Conservative candidate for constituency by-election, 1992

I don't think we want a bloody nigger to represent us.
Bill Galbraith, 1992, of John Taylor

RECESSION

Most of us have stopped using silver every day.
Margaret Thatcher

These dark days will be worth all they cost us if they teach us that our true destiny is not to be ministered unto but to minister to ourselves and to our fellow men.
Franklin D. Roosevelt

It's a recession when your neighbour loses his job; it's a depression when you lose yours.
Harry S. Truman

The loss of one's job is a misfortune which should be borne with dignity and reticence.
Norman St John-Stevas, British Conservative politician

He didn't riot. He got on his bike and looked for work.
Norman Tebbit, British Conservative politician, of his unemployed father during the Depression

Sometimes I've heard it said that Conservatives have been associated with unemployment. That's absolutely wrong. We'd have been drummed out of office if we'd had this level of unemployment.
Margaret Thatcher, May 1977, when there were 1,269,000 out of work in the UK

R E L I G I O N

Isn't God a shit!
Randolph Churchill

If men are so wicked with religion, what would they be without it?
Benjamin Franklin

Religion is by no means a proper subject of conversation in mixed company.
Lord Chesterfield

The Pope! How many divisions has he got?
Joseph Stalin (1879-1953), Soviet statesman, when urged by Pierre Laval to tolerate Catholicism in the USSR to appease the Pope, 1935

If you vote for Kinnock, you are voting against Christ.
Dame Barbara Cartland

If heaven is going to be filled with people like Hardie, well the Almighty can have them to Himself.
Sir Winston Churchill on being told that Keir Hardie would be in heaven before he would

A Catholic layman who has never been averse to giving to the Pope, or indeed anybody else who he thought might be in need of it.
Bernard Levin, of Norman St John Stevas

R E N E G A D E S

He plays the jilted Miss Haversham of the party, entangled in his own time-warp, all dressed up with nowhere to go.
Joe Joseph, The Times, 1992, of Ken Livingstone

Far from being a loony left in sheep's clothing,
Paul Boateng comes across as a sheep who used to
dress in wolf's clothing to keep up with the
fashions. He gets more sheepish by the day . . . If
Labour wins the General Election, he will
probably bleat out loud in celebration.
Joe Joseph, The Times, 1992, of Paul Boateng, Labour
MP

REPUBLICAN PARTY

The Republican Convention opened with a prayer.
If the Lord can see his way to bless the Republican
Party the way it's been carrying on, then the rest of
us ought to get it without even asking.
Will Rogers, 1928

I like Republicans, have grown up with them,
worked with them and would trust them with
anything in the world, except public office.
Adlai Stevenson

A conservative Republican is one who doesn't
believe anything new should ever be tried for the
first time. A liberal Republican is one who does
believe something should be tried for the first time
– but not now.
Mort Sahl

They've been peddling eyewash about themselves
and hogwash about the Democrats. What they
need is a good mouthwash.
Lyndon B. Johnson

It is an ancient political vehicle, held together by
soft soap and hunger and with front-seat drivers
and back-seat drivers contradicting each other in a
bedlam of voices, shouting 'go right' and 'go left'
at the same time.
Adlai Stevenson, 1952

The Republican Party either corrupts its liberals or
expels them.
Harry S. Truman

The trouble with the Republican Party is that it hasn't had a new idea for years.
Woodrow Wilson

RESIGNATIONS

I am against government by crony.
Harold L. Ickes (1874-1952), US Republican politician, commenting on his resignation as Secretary of the Interior, after a dispute with President Truman, 1946

I thought the best thing to do was to settle up these little local difficulties, and then turn to the wider vision of the Commonwealth.
Harold Macmillan, referring to resignation of ministers, 1958

When I should so much have liked to be seen as a tower of strength, I am perceived by some as a point of weakness.
David Mellor, in his resignation letter to John Major

Resignations are coming in threes – rather like packets of Mates.
Tony Banks, Labour MP, on the resignation of Michael Mates over the Nasil Nadir affair

I respect and accept your decision not to stay on.
John Major, in his letter to the resigning Chancellor, Norman Lamont

A little local difficulty.
Mr Major's response to Mr Lamont sticking the knife in, after resignation

Having consulted widely among colleagues, I have concluded that the unity of the Party and the prospects of victory in a General Election would be better served if I stood down to enable Cabinet colleagues to enter the ballot for the leadership.
Margaret Thatcher, 1990

As I look ahead, I am filled with foreboding. Like the Roman, I seem to see 'the River Tiber foaming with much blood'.
Enoch Powell, British politician, speaking of immigration in Birmingham, 1968

Why don't you resign, you plonker?
Terry Lewis, Labour MP, after the Whips announced the Government defeat over the social chapter, 1993

There is no question of anyone resigning, we are going to win this by-election.
Sir Norman Fowler, Conservative Party Chairman, when asked if he would quit if the Tories lost the Christchurch election

I was a very convenient scapegoat for many people in the party because I had resigned and was expendable.
Nigel Lawson, former Chancellor, in a television interview, October 1992

RESPONSIBILITY

Do you realise the responsibility I carry? I'm the only person standing between Nixon and the White House.
John F. Kennedy (1917-63), US statesman to Arthur Schlesinger, October 1960

Prudence is a wooden Juggernaut, before whom Benjamin Franklin walks with the portly air of a high priest.
Robert L. Stevenson

REVENGE

The American adage 'don't get mad, get even' doesn't apply to Norman. He gets mad and even.
The Observer, of Norman Tebbit

REVOLUTION

Those who make peaceful revolution impossible, make violent revolution inevitable.
John F. Kennedy, address to diplomats, 1962

We must hate – hatred is the basis of Communism. Children must be taught to hate their parents if they are not Communists.
Nikolai Lenin, Russian revolutionary leader, 1923

If you feed people just with revolutionary slogans they will listen today, they will listen tomorrow, they will listen the day after tomorrow, but on the fourth day they will say 'To hell with you!'
Nikita Khrushchev (attrib.)

If we were to promise people nothing better than only revolution, they would scratch their heads and say: 'Is it not better to have good goulash?'
Nikita Khrushchev

I have been ever of the opinion that revolutions are not to be evaded.
Benjamin Disraeli

The traditional figures of revolution, Rousseau, Karl Marx, Lenin and others, were no great emancipators of women and were themselves chauvinist. They left their wives slaving over a hot stove.
Sally Oppenheim, British Conservative politician

Revolutionaries do not make revolutions. The revolutionaries are those who know when power is lying in the street and then they can pick it up. Armed uprising by itself has never yet led to revolution.
Hannah Arendt (1906-75), American political philosopher

I should be pleased, I suppose, that Hitler has carried out a revolution on our lines. But they are Germans. So they will end by ruining our idea.
Benito Mussolini, Italian Dictator

The youth of today and of those to come after them would assess the work of the revolution in accordance with values of their own . . . a thousand years from now, all of them, even Marx, Engels, and Lenin, would possibly appear rather ridiculous.
Mao Tse-Tung

There are but three ways for the populace to escape its wretched lot. The first two are by the route of the wine shop or the church; the third is by that of the social revolution.
Michael Bakunin (1814-76), Russian Anarchist, co-founder of the First International

ROYALTY

She is a lady short on looks, absolutely deprived of any dress sense, has a figure like a Jurassic monster, is very greedy when it comes to loot, no tact and wants to upstage everyone else. I cannot think of anybody else I would sooner not appoint to this post then the Duchess of York.
Sir Nicholas Fairbairn, MP for Perth and Kinross, following revelations that the Foreign Office along with the Palace were blocking the move to appoint the Duchess of York as UN Ambassador, 1993

The charge he must answer is not that he ever arranged with the noble lords to meet around the back of a motorway service station to pick up his bung and hand over the gong. The charge is much more urbane. Word gets around that the chances of a peerage or knighthood are multiplied by generous donations.
Robin Cook, Labour Industry spokesman, on the subject of Party funding, June 1992

SANCTIONS

I totally disagree about sanctions as did the previous Labour Government and unlike him [Neil Kinnock] I am not prepared to stand there comfortably in this house and impose starvation and poverty on millions and millions of black South Africans and black children.
Margaret Thatcher, defending her opposition to sanctions against South Africa, 1988

I see history being very hard on Margaret Thatcher . . . people in the West will wake up to find their investments in South Africa on fire; unfortunately that fire will envelop us all.
Kenneth Kaunda, President of Zambia, on Mrs Thatcher's refusal to impose sanctions on South Africa during the Commonwealth conference in 1987

I am asking every country to intensify sanctions and cut diplomatic ties. Nothing has changed there to make us change our view on the policy of sanctions.
Nelson Mandela, deputy president, African National Congress, 1990

SCANDAL

There is something utterly nauseating about a system of society which pays a harlot 25 times as much as it pays its Prime Minister, 250 times as much as it pays its Members of Parliament, and 500 times as much as it pays some of its ministers of religion.
Harold Wilson, British politician and Prime Minister referring to Christine Keeler, 1963

A great party is not to be brought down because of a scandal by a woman of easy virtue and a proven liar.
Lord Hailsham, British Conservative politician, referring to the Profumo affair, 1963

He would, wouldn't he?
Mandy Rice-Davies, British call girl, of Lord Astor, when told that he had repudiated her evidence at the trial of Stephen Ward, 1963

The members of our secret service have apparently spent so much time looking under the beds for Communists, they haven't had time to look in the bed.
Michael Foot, British Labour politician, referring to the Profumo affair (attrib.)

From Lord Hailsham we have had a virtuoso performance in the art of kicking a friend in the guts. When self-indulgence has reduced a man to the shape of Lord Hailsham, sexual continence involves no more than a sense of the ridiculous.
Reginald Paget, writing about the attack on Profumo by the rotund Lord Hailsham

What have you done? cried Christine,
You've wrecked the whole party machine.
To lie in the nude may be rude,
But to lie in the House is obscene.
Anon. doggerel, quoted during the Profumo affair

Many of the scandals that I have seen have begun from glossing over unpleasant facts.
Lord Chandos (1893-1972), British industrialist, politician

I think any man in business would be foolish to fool around with his secretary. If it's somebody else's secretary, fine!
Senator Barry Goldwater

History is made in the class struggle and not in bed.
Alex Mitchell, British left-wing journalist following deposition of leader of Workers' Revolutionary Party amid sex scandal, 1985

I don't regret what I did. I had a relationship with someone I cared for deeply.
Antonia de Sancha, of her relationship with David Mellor MP, dubbed the Minister of Fun. The affair helped speed up his resignation from the post

He is a first-class barrister and was an extremely good Minister. As a son-in-law I can envisage worse.
Professor Edward Hall, father-in-law of David Mellor, following Mellor's resignation

If ever a nation was debauched by a man, the American nation has been debauched by Washington . . . If ever a nation was deceived by a man, the American nation has been deceived by Washington.
Benjamin F. Bache (1769-98), *Aurora*

Most British statesmen have either drunk too much or womanised too much. I never fell into the second category.
Lord George Brown, Labour MP

Yesterday I travelled by train, and a plump young lady came into my compartment at Waterloo. She was not wearing a bra, and her delightful globes bounced prominently, but happily, under a rope knitted jersey. After a bit I moved over and sat beside her . . . She works as a shop assistant in Maidstone.
Alan Clark MP, extract from his diaries quoted in the *Evening Standard*, 1993

As Chancellor Lamont came in from a fraternal drink with Labour's John Smith and Gordon Brown, a group of Labour MPs lustily singing broke off in mid verse and launched into *Hey Big Spender.* Norman Lamont, I am happy to say, took it all exceptionally well.
Black Dog, *Mail on Sunday*, 1992

There has always been women. He is simply an incredibly gifted vain man who cannot resist people saying he is wonderful. The girls all have their sell-by date.
Jane Clark, speaking of her husband, Alan Clark's infidelity

It's ying and yang, they really don't seem to be 'whole people' without each other. That's why I honestly don't think his sexual peccadilloes matter to them too much, except when they impact him politically.
Mary Steenburger, actress and friend of Hillary Clinton, on the Clinton's marriage

The cardinal rule of politics – never get caught in bed with a live man or a dead woman.
J. R. Ewing, Dallas

I knew about the affair . . . I told Paddy . . . 'look kiddo, you've got to come clean or people will think that it's something much worse.'
Jane Ashdown, on her husband Paddy's much publicised affair

Q. What do Gary Hart and the Boston Celtics have in common?
A. If they had played at home, they would have won.
Playboy, 1988

S E L F - K N O W L E D G E

I am the kind of woman I would run away from.
Margot Asquith

I'm not the Carter who'll never tell a lie.
Billy Carter

I may not have been a great prime minister, but I would have been a great farmer.
Golda Meir

Do I look nervous?
John Major

I'm not trying to obscure the past.
Neil Kinnock

I am my own man.
John Major, on becoming Prime Minister, 1990

SEX APPEAL SWUNG HIM INTO OVAL OFFICE

A *Today* analysis of Bill Clinton's victory shows a combination of caring policies, sex and power helped him win.

Victorious Bill Clinton hailed the women of America after their massive support put him in the White House. About 60 per cent ignored accusations of womanising and voted for him.
Today, July 1993

SOCIAL-DEMOCRATS

A Social-Democrat must never forget that the proletariat will inevitably have to wage a class struggle for Socialism even against the most democratic and republican bourgeoisie and petty bourgeoisie.
Vladimir Ilich Lenin, The State and Revolution

The heterosexual wing of the Labour Party.
George Foulkes MP

They have policies like liquid grease.
Neil Kinnock MP

Stale claret in new bottles – it is a confidence trick not to be mistaken for the elixir of life.
Francis Pym MP

SOCIALISM

We are redefining and we are restating our socialism in terms of the scientific revolution . . . the Britain that is going to be forged in the white heat of this revolution will be no place for restrictive practices or outdated methods on either side of industry.
Harold Wilson, former Labour Prime Minister, 1963

Socialism is a filthy disgusting perversion. We are the pure.
Speaker, Young Conservatives' conference, quoted in *Time Out*, 1989

My long term goal is to see Britain free from Socialism.
Margaret Thatcher

We are creeping closer to Socialism, a system that someone once said works only in Heaven where it isn't needed, and in Hell where they've already got it.
President Ronald Reagan, 1985

As far as Socialism means anything, it must be about the wider distribution of smoked salmon and caviar.
Sir Richard Marsh, former Labour Cabinet Minister

We'll find it very difficult to explain to the voters that simply by taking over Marks & Spencer we can make it as efficient as the Co-op.
Harold Wilson, 1973

Socialism can only arrive by bicycle.
Jose Antonio Viera Gallo, Chilean politician in Allende's government

In socialism there should always remain a trace of the anarchist and the libertarian, and not too much of the prig and the prude.
Anthony Crosland (1918-77), British Labour politician

Socialism proposes no adequate substitute for the motive of enlightened selfishness that today is at the basis of all human labour and effort, enterprise and new activity.
William Taft (1857-1930), American Republican politician

Socialists make the mistake of confusing individual worth with success. They believe you cannot allow people to succeed in case those who fail feel worthless.
Kenneth Baker, British Conservative politician

The inherent virtue of Socialism is the equal sharing of miseries.
Sir Winston Churchill

Socialism is Bolshevism with a shave.
Detroit Journal

I criticise doctrinaire State Socialism because it is, in fact, little better than a dusty survival of a plan to meet the problems of 50 years ago, based on a misunderstanding of what someone said 100 years ago.
Norman Mailer

As with the Christian religion, the worst advertisement for Socialism is its adherents.
George Orwell, 1937

All socialism involves slavery.
Herbert Spencer (1820-1903), English philosopher

Any man who is not something of a socialist before he is 40 has no heart. Any man who is still a socialist after he is 40 has no head.
Wendell L. Wilkie (1892-1944), US lawyer and businessman

Under socialism all will govern in turn and will soon become accustomed to no one governing.
Vladimir Ilich Lenin, The State and Revolution

State socialism is totally alien to the British character.
Margaret Thatcher, 1983

And what a prize we have to fight for: no less than the chance to banish from our land the dark divisive clouds of Marxist socialism.
Margaret Thatcher, 1983

He tended to knock off at seven o'clock – not so much a Socialist but a socialite.
Harold Wilson, of Roy Jenkins

SPEAKERS AND
SPEECHES

I stand up when he nudges me. I sit down when they pull my coat.
Ernest Bevin, Labour politician

The human brain starts working the moment you are born and never stops until you stand up to speak in public.
Sir George Jessel, judge, MP, solicitor-general and Master of the Rolls

A toastmaster is a man who eats a meal he doesn't want so he can get up and tell a lot of stories he doesn't remember to people who've already heard them.
Sir George Jessel MP

A speech is like a love affair. Any fool can start it, but to end it requires considerable skill.
Lord Mancroft

The last time I was in this hall was when my late beloved boss, Frank Knox, the Secretary of the Navy, spoke here, and it was a better speech he gave then than the one I'll be giving tonight. I know. I wrote them both.
Adlai Stevenson

The Right Honourable and Learned Gentleman has twice crossed the floor of this House, each time leaving behind a trail of slime.
David Lloyd George of Sir John Simon, 1931

I think this is the most extraordinary collection of talent, of human knowledge, that has ever been gathered together at the White House – with the possible exception of when Thomas Jefferson dined alone.
John F. Kennedy, at White House dinner honouring Nobel prize winners, 1962

Most people have ears, but few have judgment; tickle those ears, and, depend upon it, you will catch their judgments, such as they are.
Lord Chesterfield (1694-1773), English statesman

He can best be described as one of those orators who, before they get up, do not know what they are going to say; when they are speaking, do not know what they are saying; and, when they have sat down, do not know what they have said.
Sir Winston Churchill

All you need to do to get a speech out of Mr Choate is to open his mouth, drop in a dinner, and up comes a speech.
Chauncey Depew (1834-1928), American Republican politician, of Ambassador Joseph H. Choate

I do not object to people looking at their watches when I am speaking. But I strongly object when they start shaking them to make certain they are still going.
Lord Birkett (1883-1962), British lawyer, Liberal politician

Giving a speech is like sex. You're supposed to be exhausted when you're done.
Vernon Jordan, Clinton adviser

The bestial nature of the indecent horde of pirates, second-storey men, porch climbers, gunmen and short card dealers who oppose me is now perfectly manifest.
Parody of a Roosevelt campaign speech

The effect of Hewson's speeches was like being flogged by a warm lettuce.
Paul Keating, of his political opponent, John Hewson

I never rated Kinnock as anything but a windbag whose incoherent speeches spring from an incoherent mind.
Norman Tebbit

He did more harm to British industry in one speech than the combined efforts of the Luftwaffe and U-Boats did in the whole of the last War.
Cyril Smith, of Tony Benn

He talks so fast that listening to him is like trying to read *Playboy* magazine with your wife turning the pages.
Barry Goldwater, of Hubert H. Humphrey

Ed Muskie talked like a farmer with terminal cancer trying to borrow on next year's crop.
Hunter S. Thomson, Fear and Loathing on the Campaign Trail, 1972

S T A R S

Modesty forbids me to answer.
Denis Healey, Labour politician, on being asked who was the greatest prime minister Britain ever had, 1993

If Clinton had a choice of meeting Maggie Thatcher to discuss world affairs or Barbra Streisand, there is no doubt which one he would choose. It would be Streisand every time. He's fixated on Hollywood and its celebrities.
Tony Burton, New York columnist, 1993

The radiation and vitality was such that you felt electrified by it. But you also felt uncertain, you didn't know what was going to happen next. I never felt that with any other minister or any other member of the Government; I couldn't give a damn what they wanted. But with her, I wished to please her, and not for my own advancement. I wished to please her because she was such a remarkable individual.
Alan Clark, former Defence Minister, referring to Margaret Thatcher, 1993

Arriving with all the urgency of Dyno-Rod to the scene of a drain-clearing emergency, the Smiling-Talking-Greeting-Walking-Living-Photo-Opportunity Mr Heseltine descended on Forest Hill . . . a rising Conservative star should think twice before acting with children, animals and Michael Heseltine.
Joe Joseph, journalist, of Michael Heseltine, 1992

He would swim through shark-infested water to get near a microphone.
Jeremy Paxman, television presenter, interviewer, of MP Teddy Taylor

We should really call all politicians actors.
Marlon Brando, Newsweek, 1972

We vote for a person: 'Seems like he's got integrity.'
An actor is trained for a long time to fake integrity.
Dustin Hoffman

May I say that as long as actors are going into politics, I wish for Christ's sake that Sean Connery would become King of Scotland.
John Huston (1906-87), *Rolling Stone*, 1981

STATE

The State is made for man, not man for the State.
Albert Einstein (1879-1955), German-born mathematical physicist, *The World as I See It*

STATISTICS

There are three kinds of lies: lies, damned lies, and statistics.
Benjamin Disraeli

Statistics are like alienists – they will testify for either side.
Fiorello La Guardia (1882-1947), American politician, Mayor of New York

STRIKES

The General Strike has taught the working class more in four days than years of talking could have done.
A. J. Balfour (1848-1930), British Conservative politician, Prime Minister

We had to fight the enemy without in the Falklands. We always have to be aware of the enemy within, which is more difficult to fight and more dangerous to liberty.
Margaret Thatcher, on the 1984-85 miners' strike, 1984

Beer and sandwiches at No. 10? No, never.
Margaret Thatcher, rejecting the idea of Downing Street negotiations to end the miners' strike of 1984-85, 1984

I'm not a very pleasant gentleman when the chips are down and I know how to put the boot in as well as anybody.
Joe Gormley, former president, National Union of Mineworkers, 1982

I do enjoy it, it gees me up. The blood rises once they start on me.
Eric Hammond, moderate general secretary, Electrical Electronic, Telecommunications and Plumbing Union, on the heckling he attracts from the Left at conferences and meetings, 1986

When the Queen invests him, she should bring the sword down with a horizontal movement across the shoulders, perhaps with a little flick of the wrist.
Peter Heathfield, General Secretary, National Union of Mineworkers, on Sir Ian MacGregor, former chairman, National Coal Board, 1986

S T Y L E

In debate, his method is rather akin to the manner
of a Shakespearean actor auditioning for a crowd
scene at a football match.
Greg Knight, of Andrew Faulds

Michael Heseltine put the con into conservative
and John Major put the er... er in.
Neil Kinnock, 1992

Being attacked in the House by him is like being
savaged by a dead sheep.
Denis Healey, 1978, of Geoffrey Howe

S U C C E S S

You never learn from success. Success you take as
the natural order of things.
Lord Young of Graffham, former Secretary of State for
Trade and Industry, 1985

I can honestly say that I was never affected by the
question of the success of an undertaking. If I felt
it was the right thing to do, I was for it regardless
of the possible outcome.
Golda Meir, Russian-born Israeli stateswoman

The most successful politician is he who says what
everybody is thinking most often and in the
loudest voice.
Theodore Roosevelt

Too many people have forgotten that it was he
who led us to an election victory last year that
many thought impossible.
Ian Lang, Scottish Secretary, on criticism of John Major,
1993

The best immediate defence of the United States is
the success of Great Britain defending itself.
Franklin D. Roosevelt, 1940

The penalty of success is to be bored by people
who used to snub you.
Nancy Astor, 1956

This is the victory for the true believers!
Paul Keating, Australian Labour MP, on his being
elected Labour Leader, 1993

What I don't understand, is why a complete wimp
like me keeps winning.
John Major, 1993

This is a great day for Denmark. All the Danish
requests have been satisfied.
Poul Schluter, Danish Prime Minister, EEC Summit, 1992

SURVIVAL

If you live among wolves you have to act like a
wolf.
Nikita Khrushchev

Once one determines that he or she has a mission
in life, that it's not going to be accomplished
without a great deal of pain and that the rewards
in the end may not outweigh the pain – if you
recognise historically that always happens, then
when it comes, you survive it.
Richard Nixon

Nothing in life is so exhilarating as to be shot at
without result.
Sir Winston Churchill

TAXATION

The taxpayer – that's someone who works for the
federal government but doesn't have to take a civil
service exam.
Ronald Reagan

I warn you, there are going to be howls of anguish
from the 80,000 people who are rich enough to
pay over 57 per cent on the last slice of their
income.
Denis Healey MP, then Shadow Chancellor of the
Exchequer, on the Labour Party's plan to increase taxation,
1973

Taxes, after all, are the dues we pay for the privileges of membership in an organised society.
Franklin D. Roosevelt, 1936

You don't make the poor rich by making the rich poor.
Nigel Lawson MP, when Chancellor of the Exchequer, quoting Prof. Baron Bauer, economist, 1987

Read my lips: no new taxes.
George Bush, promise made during the 1988 United States presidential campaign

The art of taxation consists in so plucking the goose as to obtain the largest amount of feathers with the least amount of hissing.
Jean Baptiste Colbert (1619-83), French statesman

To tax and to please, no more than to love and to
be wise, is not given to men.
Edmund Burke (1729-97), Irish philosopher, statesman

We are looking for a wealth tax that will bring in
sufficient revenue to justify having a wealth tax.
Dick Spring, leader of Irish Labour Party, 1982

Taxes cause crime. When the tax rate reaches 25
per cent, there is an increase in lawlessness.
America's tax system is inspired by Karl Marx.
Ronald Reagan

The entire graduated income tax structure was
created by Karl Marx.
Ronald Reagan

TELEVISION

Television is a penny Punch and Judy show.
Sir Winston Churchill

No TV performance takes such careful preparation
as an off-the-cuff talk-show.
Richard Nixon

TERRORISM

A little group of wilful men reflecting no opinion
but their own have rendered the great Government
of the United States helpless and contemptible.
Woodrow Wilson

After seeing Rambo last night I know what to do
next time this happens.
Ronald Reagan, following the interception of the plane
carrying the hijackers of the Achille Lauro cruise-ship,
1985

No one can kill Americans and brag about it.
No one.
Ronald Reagan, after the attack on Libya, 1986

THIRD WORLD

Where there are two PhDs in a developing country, one is Head of State and the other is in exile.
Lord Samuel (1898-1978), British administrator, author

The Third World is not a reality, but an ideology.
Hannah Arendt (1906-75), American political philosopher

Our mistake was in the assumption that freedom – real freedom – would necessarily and with little trouble follow liberation from alien rule . . . Our countries are effectively being governed by people who have only the most marginal interest in our affairs.
Julius Nyerere, African statesman, President of Tanzania

A nation's strength ultimately consists in what it can do on its own, and not in what it can borrow from others.
Indira Gandhi (1917-1984)

TIME

We must use time as a tool, not as a couch.
John F. Kennedy

I recommend you to take care of the minutes: for hours will take care of themselves.
Lord Chesterfield

An hour is a long time in politics.
Jack Cunningham MP, 1993

TRADE UNIONS

SHOP STEWARD: From now on all wages are doubled, holidays are increased to twelve weeks and we shall only work Fridays?
Guardian newspaper

MINISTER OF LABOUR: . . . The workers of Freedonia are demanding shorter hours.
FIREFLY (GROUCHO MARX): Very well, we'll give them shorter hours. We'll start by cutting their lunch hour to twenty minutes.
Arthur Sheekman and Nat Perrin, Duck Soup, screenplay, 1933

I see no need for a Royal Commission [on trades unions] which will take minutes and waste years.
Harold Wilson, 1964

The history of all countries shows that the working class, exclusively by its own effort, is able to develop only trade union consciousness.
Vladimir Ilyich Lenin

Solidarity still exists inside us, even in those who deny it.
Lech Walesa

It obviously hurt him to wear the dinner jacket of respectability instead of the boilersuit of revolt.
Cassandra, of Ted Hill, leader of the Boilermakers' Union

Gompers says that strikes are a blessing to society. Must be one of those blessings in disguise.
Nashville Southern Lumberman of Samuel Gompers, American Union leader

Jimmy Hoffa's most valuable contribution to the American labour movement came at the moment he stopped breathing on July 30, 1975.
Dan E. Moldea, of Jimmy Hoffa, American Union leader, 1978

You are like a nightingale. It closes its eyes when it sings and sees nothing and hears nobody except itself.
Nikita Khruschev of Walter Reuther, American Union leader

Unions run by workers are like alcoholic homes run by alcoholics, a sure recipe for tyranny.
Roy Kerridge, 1984

Unionism seldom, if ever, uses such power as it has to insure better work; almost always it devotes a large part of that power to safeguarding bad work.
H. L. Mencken, 1922

Unions are getting such a bad name, it's no wonder they're called Brother Hoods.
Robert Orben

He suffered more than any other trade union leader from the malady known as enuresis – a propensity for leaking when Pressmen are present.
Harold Wilson, on Tom O'Brien, leader of the N.A.C.E.

T R E A T I E S

Treaties are like roses and young girls – they last while they last.
Charles de Gaulle (attrib.)

I bear solemn witness to the fact that NATO heads of state and of government meet only to go through the tedious motions of reading speeches, drafted by others, with the principal activity of not rocking the boat.
Pierre Trudeau, of NATO

T R I B U T E

. . . that great lover of peace, a man of giant stature who moulded, as few other men have done, the destinies of his age.
Jawaharlal Nehru (1889-1964), First Indian Prime Minister, referring to Stalin, Obituary tribute, 1953

She would rather light candles than curse the darkness, and her glow has warmed the world.
Adlai Stevenson, US statesman, referring to Eleanor Roosevelt, who had recently died, 1962

You could wipe the floor with the lot of 'em.
Michael Cartiss MP, shouting support for Margaret Thatcher during her last performance in the chamber, 1990

A piece of each of us died at that moment.
Michael J. Mansfield, US senator, referring to the
assassination of President Kennedy, 1963

TRUTH

To become properly acquainted with a truth we
must first have disbelieved it, and disputed against
it.
Prince Otto von Bismarck, Prussian statesman

Men occasionally stumble over the truth, but most
of them pick themselves up and hurry off as if
nothing had happened.
Sir Winston Churchill

Truth is so important that it needs to be
surrounded by a bodyguard of lies.
George Shultz, American Republican politician,
Secretary of State, on the disinformation campaign against
Libya, 1986

If you ever injected truth into politics you would
have no politics.
Will Rogers

Let us begin by committing ourselves to the truth,
to see it like it is and to tell it like it is, to find the
truth, to speak the truth and live with the truth.
That's what we'll do.
Richard Nixon, Nomination acceptance speech, 1968

It is simply untrue that all our institutions are evil,
that all adults are unsympathetic, that all politicians
are mere opportunists, that all aspects of university
life are corrupt. Having discovered an illness, it's
not terribly useful to prescribe death as a cure.
Senator George McGovern

A truism is on that account none the less true.
Herbert Samuel, A Book of Quotations

I never trust a man unless I've got his pecker in my
pocket.
Lyndon B. Johnson

If it barks and has a tail I know it's a dog, but no doubt your smart statisticians in the Conservative Central Office would tell me it's a kangaroo with an attitude problem.
Brian Bethell, to Michael Heseltine on BBC's *Election Call*

I am sure Mr Heath thinks he is so honest. But I wish he didn't have to have his friends say it so often.
Roy Jenkins, 1970, of Edward Heath

UNEMPLOYMENT

He didn't riot. He got on his bike and looked for work.
Norman Tebbit MP, then Secretary of State for Employment, on his father, 1981

I would feel desperate if I had been without a good regular income for 20 weeks.
Margaret Thatcher, 1984

Wanting to work is so rare a want that it should be encouraged.
Abraham Lincoln

UNITED NATIONS

If the UN is a country unto itself, then the commodity it exports most is words.
Edna B. Fein, *The New York Times,* 1985

This organisation is created to prevent you from going to hell. It isn't created to take you to heaven.
Henry Cabot Lodge Jr

The UN cannot do anything, and never could; it is not an animate entity or agent. It is a place, a stage, a forum and a shrine . . . a place to which powerful people can repair when they are fearful about the course on which their own rhetoric seems to be propelling them.
Conor Cruise O'Brien, *New Republic,* 1985

The UN is a temple to Parkinson's Law – where inefficiency and extravagance worship at its shrines and hypocrisy at its altars.
R. J. Turnbull, 1970

New York would rather be the permanent home of the World Series than capital of the League of Nations
Vancouver Province

UNITED STATES OF AMERICA

I was born an American; I will live an American; I shall die an American.
Daniel Webster (1782-1852), US Statesman, 1850

Whatever America hopes to bring to pass in this world must first come to pass in the heart of America.
Dwight D. Eisenhower, US General and statesman, 1953

I'd rather trust the government of the USA to the first 400 people listed in the Boston telephone directory than to the faculty of Harvard University.
William Buckley Jnr

No man should be in public office who can't make more money in private life.
Thomas E. Dewey

America is still a government of the naive, for the naive, by the naive.
Christopher Morley, Inward Ho! 1923

You can always get the truth from an American statesman after he has turned seventy or given up all hope of the Presidency.
Wendel Phillips

Ninety-eight per cent of the adults in this country are decent, hard-working, honest Americans. It's the other lousy two per cent that gets all the publicity. But then – we elected them.
Lily Tomlin

The United States is like a gigantic boiler. Once the fire is lighted under it there is no limit to the power it can generate.
Viscount Edward Grey (1862-1933), British statesman

Double – no triple – our troubles and we'd still be better off than any other people on earth.
Ronald Reagan

In the field of world policy; I would dedicate this nation to the policy of the good neighbour.
Franklin D. Roosevelt, First Inaugural Address, 1933

THE USSR

No nation has ever devoured its heroes with such primordial zest.
Cassandra, British journalist

The Union of Soviet Socialist Republics is not just a country, but an empire – the largest, and probably the last, in history.
Time magazine, 1980

The Soviet Union will remain a one-party nation even if an opposition party were permitted – because everyone would join that party.
Ronald Reagan

In the Soviet Union everything happens slowly. Always remember that.
A. N. Shevchenko, defecting Soviet diplomat

If we are going in without the help of Russia we are walking into a trap.
David Lloyd George, in a speech to the House of Commons, 1939
Our achievements leave class enemies breathless.
Leonid Brezhnev (1906-82), Soviet leader

Give us time and we shall produce panties for your wives in colours which cannot be seen anywhere else.
Nikita Khrushchev

V I E T N A M

The U.S. has broken the second rule of war. That is, don't go fighting with your land army on the mainland of Asia. Rule One is don't march on Moscow. I developed these two rules myself.
Viscount Montgomery of Alamein (1887-1976), British Field Marshal, Deputy Commander of NATO forces

We are all the President's men.
Henry Kissinger, German born US politician and diplomat, regarding the invasion of Cambodia, quoted in the *Sunday Times Magazine,* 1975

It is worse than immoral, it's a mistake.
Dean Acheson, lawyer and statesman, describing the Vietnam war

Bombing can end the war – bomb the Pentagon now!
Graffito, New York, 1970

Draft Beer, Not Students.
Badge slogan

This is not a jungle war, but a struggle for freedom on every front of human activity.
Lyndon B. Johnson

North Vietnam cannot defeat or humiliate the United States. Only Americans can do that.
Richard Nixon, 1969

I would like to ask a question. Would this sort of war or savage bombing which has taken place in Vietnam have been tolerated for so long had the people been European?
Indira Gandhi

The conventional army loses if it does not win. The guerrilla wins if he does not lose.
Henry Kissinger, Foreign Affairs, 1969

VIRTUE

There are few virtues that the Poles do not possess – and there are few mistakes they have ever avoided.
Winston Churchill, 1945

VITRIOL

Peel's smile: like the silver plate on a coffin.
Daniel O'Connell (1775-1847), Irish politician, referring to Sir Robert Peel; quoting J. P. Curran, 1835

A lot of people misunderstand Barry. But actually, when you get to know him, he's quite reactionary.
Abu, of Senator Goldwater

You snivelling little git.
Brian Sedgemore MP to Nigel Lawson MP, then Chancellor of the Exchequer, during a debate on the Johnson Mathey Bank scandal, 1985

To call you a pest would be unfair to pests.
Nigel Lawson MP, ripostes, 1985

She is the Enid Blyton of economics. Nothing must be allowed to spoil her simple plots.
Lord Holme, former president, Liberal Party, on Margaret Thatcher, 1980

Gladstone, like Richelieu, can't write. Nothing can be more unmusical, more involved or more uncouth than all his scribblement.
Benjamin Disraeli (1804-81), British statesman, 1877

Their worst misfortune was his birth; their next worst – his death.
Sir Winston Churchill, British Statesman, referring to Lenin, 1924

Greater love hath no man than this, that he lay down his friends for his life.
Jeremy Thorpe, British politician, after Macmillan's Cabinet reshuffle, 1962

How could they tell?
Dorothy Parker (1893-1967), US writer, on the news of the death of Calvin Coolidge, US President 1923-29, *You Might As Well Live*

Sit down, man. You're a bloody tragedy.
James Maxton (1885-1946), Scottish Labour leader, to Ramsay MacDonald when he made his last speech in Parliament (attrib.)

Simply a radio personality who outlived his prime.
Evelyn Waugh (1903-66), British novelist, referring to Winston Churchill

It is fitting that we should have buried the Unknown Prime Minister by the side of the Unknown Soldier.
Lord Asquith, of Bonar Law, British Prime Minister, 1922

When they circumcised Herbert Samuel, they threw away the wrong bit.
David Lloyd George, on his fellow Liberal, 1930s

. . . when political ammunition runs low, inevitably the rusty artillery of abuse is always wheeled into action.
Adlai Stevenson, 1952

Sir Alec Douglas-Home, when he was a British Foreign Secretary said he received the following telegram from an irate citizen: 'To hell with you. Offensive letter follows.'
William Safire, The New Language of Politics, 1968

A statesman is a politician who's been dead ten or fifteen years.
Harry S. Truman, quoted in *New York World-Telegram,* 1958

. . . like being savaged by a dead sheep.
Denis Healey, on Geoffrey Howe's attack on his budget, 1978

You're not an MP, you're a gastronomic pimp.
Aneurin Bevan, British Labour politician, to a colleague accused of attending too many public dinners

You are a silly, crude bitch and since you are a potential breeder, God help the next generation.
Sir Nicholas Fairbairn, Tory MP, to a young woman heckler

That dirty little atheist.
Theodore Roosevelt, of Thomas Paine

I don't see much future for the Americans . . . Everything about the behaviour of American society reveals that it's half judaised, and the other half negrified. How can one expect a state like that to hold together?
Adolf Hitler

America is the only nation in history which miraculously has gone directly from barbarism to degeneration without the usual interval of civilisation.
George Clemenceau

McKinley has a chocolate-éclair backbone.
Theodore Roosevelt, on William E. McKinley

This little flower, this delicate little beauty, this cream puff is supposed to be beyond criticism . . . He is simply a shiver looking for a spine to run up.
John Hewson, Liberal National Party Leader, of his opponent, Paul Keating, 1993

I think in all fairness to the man, you'd have to put him right up there with Judas Iscariot.
G. Gordon Liddy, of John W. Dean, Counsel to President Nixon

A mythical person first thought up by the *Reader's Digest.*
Art Buchwald, of J. Edgar Hoover, Head of the FBI

A pimp and a bastard.
Aneurin Bevan, of George Brown

A semi-house-trained polecat.
Michael Foot, of Teddy Taylor

'Shinbad the Tailor' is by far the least attractive member of the government, always looking round for someone to whom to pass the blame. He will not face facts squarely. He is a coarse-grained shit and a low cur.
Hugh Dalton, of Emmanuel (Manny) Shinwell

He greets every problem head on – with an open mouth and a closed mind. He gives an impression of a mixture between Uriah Heep and Jaws. He has about as much charm as a puff adder.
John Major, of David Winnick

W A R

The ballot is stronger than the bullet.
Abraham Lincoln, 1856

If you don't want to use the army, I should like to borrow it for a while. Yours respectfully,
A. Lincoln.
Abraham Lincoln in a letter to General George B. McClellan, whose lack of activity during the US Civil War irritated Lincoln

Military glory is the attractive rainbow that rises in showers of blood.
Abraham Lincoln

If, therefore, war should ever come between these two countries, which Heaven forbid! it will not, I think, be due to irresistible natural laws, it will be due to the want of human wisdom.
Andrew Bonar Law, British statesman, referring to the UK and Germany, 1911

War is the continuation of politics. In this sense war is politics and war itself is a political action.
Mao Tse-Tung (1893-1976), Chinese Communist leader, *Quotations from Chairman Mao Tse-Tung*

To jaw-jaw is better than to war-war.
Sir Winston Churchill, British statesman, in Washington, 1954

The lamps are going out all over Europe; we shall not see them lit again in our lifetime.
Lord Grey of Falloden (1862-1933), British statesman, 1914

History shows that there are no invincible armies.
Joseph Stalin

We are advocates of the abolition of war, we do not want war; but war can only be abolished through war, and in order to get rid of the gun it is necessary to take up the gun.
Mao Tse-Tung, Quotations from Chairman Mao Tse-Tung

Older men declare war. But it is youth that must fight and die.
Herbert Hoover, US statesman and Republican President, 1944

They have caused Egypt to stagger as a drunken man staggereth in his vomit.
David Ben Gurion (1886-1973), Israeli statesman, of the Israeli army in the 1956 Suez campaign

No one hates war more than one who has seen a lot of it.
Richard Nixon, 1959

History is littered with wars which everybody knew would never happen.
Enoch Powell

The war has already almost destroyed that nation . . . I have seen, I guess, as much blood and disaster as any living man and it just turned my stomach the last time I was there. After I looked at that wreckage and those thousands of women and children and everything, I vomited.
General MacArthur (1880-1964), of the Korean war

I have nothing to offer but blood, toil, tears and sweat.
Sir Winston Churchill

And while I am talking to you mothers and fathers, I give you one more assurance. I have said this before, but I shall say it again and again and again: Your boys are not going to be sent into any foreign wars.
Franklin D. Roosevelt, 1940

If both sides don't want war, how can war break out?
Menachem Begin, Israeli politician, Prime Minister, 1981

More than an end to war, we want an end to the beginnings of all wars.
Franklin D. Roosevelt

Of the four wars in my lifetime, none came about because the US was too strong.
Ronald Reagan

My views with regard to war are well known. I grew up in a tradition where we consider all wars immoral.
Richard Nixon

They talk about who won and who lost.
Human reason won. Mankind won.
Nikita Khrushchev, of the Cuban missile crisis, 1962

I have spent much of my life fighting the Germans and fighting the politicians. It is much easier to fight the Germans.
Field Marshal Lord Montgomery, 1967

We have been a little like an accomplice to massacre. We cannot carry on like that.
Margaret Thatcher on the West's role in Bosnia

. . . Emotional nonsense.
Malcolm Rifkind, Defence Secretary, reply to her comments, 1993

The United States must be neutral in fact as well as in name during these days that are to try men's souls. We must be impartial in thought as well as in action.
Woodrow Wilson, US statesman, 1914

The maxim of the British people is 'Business as usual'.
Sir Winston Churchill, British statesman, 1914

Don't talk to me about naval tradition. It's nothing but rum, sodomy, and the lash.
Sir Winston Churchill

America . . . is the prize amateur nation in the world. Germany is the prize professional nation.
Woodrow Wilson, US statesman

My home policy? I wage war. My foreign policy? I wage war. Always, everywhere, I wage war . . . And I shall continue to wage war until the last quarter of an hour.
George Clemenceau (1841-1929), French statesman, 1918

A lot of hard-faced men who look as if they had done very well out of the war.
Stanley Baldwin, British statesman, referring to the first House of Commons elected after World War I, 1918

I fear we have only awakened a sleeping giant, and his reaction will be terrible.
Isoroku Yamamoto (1884-1943), Japanese admiral, after the Japanese attack on Pearl Harbor, 1941

A prisoner of war is a man who tries to kill you and fails, and then asks you not to kill him.
Sir Winston Churchill, 1952

Nothing in life is so exhilarating as to be shot at without result.
Sir Winston Churchill, The Malakand Field Force, 1898

Don't tread on us.
Bill Clinton, warning to Iraqi leader Saddam Hussein, following the American missile attack on Baghdad in retaliation for an alleged plot to assassinate George Bush, 1993

I fired him because he wouldn't respect the
authority of the President. That's the answer to
that. I didn't fire him because he was a dumb son
of a bitch, although he was, but that's not against
the law for generals. If it was, half to three-
quarters of them would be in jail.
Harry S. Truman, on his sacking of General MacArthur
as Commander-in-Chief of the US forces in Korea, 1951

War will exist until that distant day when the
conscientious objector enjoys the same reputation
and prestige that the warrior does today.
John F. Kennedy

War can only be abolished through war.
Mao Tse-Tung

In time of war the loudest patriots are the greatest
profiteers.
August Bebel (1840-1913), German Socialist politician,
and Co-founder of the German Social Democratic Party,
God and The State, 1882

Defeat of Germany means the defeat of Japan,
probably without firing a shot or losing a life.
Franklin D. Roosevelt, The Hinge of Fate

The tasks of the party are . . . to be cautious and
not allow our country to be drawn into conflicts
by warmongers who are accustomed to have
others pull the chestnuts out of the fire for them.
Joseph Stalin, 1941

Because you can't help everybody, doesn't mean
you can't help somebody.
Douglas Hurd on the decision to bring five-year-old
Irma Hadzimuratovic, wounded in Sarajevo, to London for
medical treatment

Must we put on a theatre to save the other
people's lives? We can save an awful lot of lives
here, if we get the electricity.
Dr Vesna Cengic, who treated Irma, on the UN
operation to evacuate the sick and wounded from Sarajevo

If a single NATO bomb strikes a Serbian position,
there will be no more talks.
Radovan Karadzio, Bosnian Serb leader

Sir: Your coverage of the Falklands episode has cleared up one small point: whether you run a fairly responsible journal of the libertarian Right or a fairly entertaining magazine. However, there are so few of these about nowadays that I am probably justified in keeping up my subscription, though I suppose it is a bit frivolous of me.
Kingsley Amis, letter to the *Spectator*, 1982

From Michael Foot's statements, one would draw the conclusion that Labour is in favour of warmongering, provided there is no war.
Labour Herald, 1982, referring to the Falkland crisis

The conflict over the Falklands is a moment dislodged from its natural home in the late nineteenth century.
Lance Morrow, 1982

This has been a pimple on the ass of progress festering for 200 years, and I guess someone decided to lance it.
Alexander Haig, US Secretary of State, on the Falkland Islands, 1982

I'm thoroughly in favour of Mrs Thatcher's visit to the Falklands. I find a bit of hesitation, though, about her coming back.
John Mortimer, *Any Questions*

Saddam Insane is the SCUD of the Earth!
Colin M. Jarman, of Saddam Hussein, Iraqi Commander-in-Chief, 1991

As far as Saddam Hussein being a great military strategist, he is neither a strategist, nor is he schooled in operational arts. He's not a tactician. He's not a general. He's not a soldier. Other than that, he's a great military man.
General H. Norman Schwarzkopf, 1991

WASHINGTON

When I first went to Washington, I thought, what is li'l ole me doing with these ninety-nine great people? Now I ask myself, what am I doing with these ninety-nine jerks?
S. I. Hayakawa, US Senator

I love to go to Washington – if only to be near my money.
Bob Hope, American actor, comedian

I find in Washington that when you ask what time it is you get different answers from Democrats and Republicans; 435 answers from the House of Representatives; a 500 page report from some consultants on how to tell time; no answer from your lawyer and a bill for $1,000.
R. Tim McNamara, Deputy Secretary of the Treasury under President Reagan

Washington is the only place where sound travels faster than light.
C. V. R. Thompson, Reader's Digest, 1949

The District of Columbia is a territory hounded on all sides by the United States of America.
Irving D. Tressler, Reader's Digest, 1949

Every man who takes office in Washington either grows or swells, and when I give a man an office, I watch him carefully to see whether he is swelling or growing.
Woodrow Wilson

WATERGATE

Dick Nixon before he dicks you.
Car sticker, Washington 1974

I suppose we should all sing 'Bail to the Chief'.
Howard Baker, Republican senator, 1974

If [President Nixon's secretary] Rosemary Woods had been Moses' secretary, there would be only eight commandments.
Art Buchwald, 1974

... we've passed from the age of the common man to the common crook.
J. K. Galbraith, 1974

A group of politicians deciding to dump a President because his morals are bad is like the Mafia getting together to bump off the Godfather for not going to church on Sunday.
Russell Baker, *New York Times,* 1974

The best time to listen to a politician is when he's on a stump on a street corner in the rain late at night when he's exhausted. Then he doesn't lie.
Theodore White, *New York Times,* 1969

WESTMINSTER

Politicians make good company for a while just as children do – their self-enjoyment is contagious. But they soon exhaust their favourite subjects – themselves.
Gary Wills

This place is a ridiculous madhouse seemingly invented by Kafka. You start work at 2.30 in the afternoon and you finish at 10 at night. It is an institution deliberately designed to give MPs the earliest possible heart attack, to deny them any social life and to smash up their marriages.
Paddy Ashdown, Liberal Democrat leader, 1992

WHITEHALL

Removing regulation from Whitehall is like wrestling with a greasy pig.
John Major, 1993

THE WHITE HOUSE

A few more fat, old bald men wouldn't hurt the place.
Marlin Fitzwater on inexperience in the White House

If you want a friend in Washington – get yourself a dog.
Harry S. Truman

I spent about 15 minutes with Jimmy Carter in the White House. God, I was uncomfortable. But that's my problem, not his.
Paul Newman, Rolling Stone, 1983

W I S D O M

The best way I know of to win an argument is to start by being in the right.
Quentin Hogg MP

An appeaser is one who feeds a crocodile – hoping that it will eat him last.
Sir Winston Churchill (attrib.)

One fifth of the people are against everything all the time.
Robert Kennedy, US politician, 1964

I'd much rather have that fellow inside my tent pissing out, than outside my tent pissing in.
Lyndon B. Johnson, US statesman, when asked why he retained J. Edgar Hoover at the FBI, 1971

I believe the greatest asset a head of state can have is the ability to get a good night's sleep.
Harold Wilson, British politician and prime minister, 1975

The great enemy of the truth is very often not the lie – deliberate, contrived and dishonest – but the myth – persistent, persuasive and unrealistic.
John F. Kennedy

There are moments in history when brooding tragedy and its dark shadows can be lightened by recalling great moments of the past.
Indira Gandhi, in a letter to Richard Nixon, 1971

No one can make you feel inferior without your consent.
Eleanor Roosevelt, writer and lecturer, wife of Franklin D. Roosevelt

I think if the people of this country can be reached with the truth, their judgment will be in favour of the many, as against the privileged few.
Eleanor Roosevelt, *Ladies' Home Journal*

Hansard is history's ear, already listening.
Herbert Samuel, 1949

Most people seek after what they do not possess and are enslaved by the very things they want to acquire.
Anwar El-Sadat

W I T

A witty thing never excites laughter; it pleases only the mind and never distorts the countenance.
Lord Chesterfield

Well, I find that a change of nuisances is as good as a vacation.
David Lloyd George, when asked how he maintained his cheerfulness when beset by numerous political obstacles

Hegel says somewhere that all great events and personalities in world history reappear in one fashion or another. He forgot to add: the first time as tragedy, the second as farce.
Karl Marx, *The Eighteenth Brumaire of Louis Napoleon*

The world is becoming like a lunatic asylum run by lunatics.
David Lloyd George, 1935

The trouble with Senator Long is that he is suffering from halitosis of the intellect. That's presuming Emperor Long has an intellect.
Harold L. Ickes, *The Politics of Upheaval*

Politics is developing more comedians than radio ever did.
Jimmy Durante

A mugwump is one of those boys who always has his mug on one side of the political fence and his wump on the other.
Albert J. Engel, 1936

Politicians as a class radiate a powerful odour.
Their business is almost as firmly grounded on
false pretences as that of the quack doctor or the
shyster lawyer.
H. L. Mencken, 1924

Two members of the acting profession who are not
needed by that profession, Mr Ronald Reagan and
Mr George Murphy, entered politics and they've
done extremely well. Since there has been no
reciprocal tendency in the other direction, it
suggests to me that an actor's job is still more
difficult than their new one.
Peter Ustinov

On the rhinoceros – here is an animal with a hide
two feet thick, and no apparent interest in politics.
What a waste.
James C. Wright, New York Times, 1986

A statesman is an easy man,
He tells his lies by rote;
A journalist makes up his lies
And takes you by the throat;
So stay at home and drink your beer
And let the neighbours vote.
William B. Yeats, The Old Stone Cross

Impossible to be present for the first performance.
Will attend the second – if there is one.
Sir Winston Churchill, declining the offer to attend a
theatre 'first night'

I'm waiting for the cock to crow.
William Morris Hughes (1864-1952), Australian
statesman and Prime Minister, said in parliament, after
being viciously criticised by a member of his own party

I do not object to Gladstone's always having the
ace of trumps up his sleeve, but only to his
pretence that God had put it there.
Henry Labouchere (1798-1869), British statesman
(attrib.)

I am painted as the greatest little dictator, which is
ridiculous – you always take some consultations.
Margaret Thatcher, 1983

What satirist ever toppled the Government? Swift managed to get one small tax law changed in his whole career.
Ian Hislop, editor *Private Eye,* 1993

He behaves like an agitated parrot with constipation. He is more funny than wise.
John Major, Conservative Prime Minister of Frank Dobson

WOMEN

I use to be in favour of women priests but two years in the Cabinet cured me of them.
Norman St John-Stevas, ex-member of Mrs Thatcher's Government, 1981

I've lost count of the times I've been invited to functions with the instructions to wear a lounge suit and bring my wife. One of these days I just might.
Angela Eagle, Labour MP, 1993

The idea that there are women who run perfect homes and have delightful children who never get chickenpox without giving a month's notice is unrealistic.
Angela Browning, Conservative MP, 1993

Often women have babies because they can't think of anything better to do.
Lord Beaumont of Whitley, British prelate, politician, journalist

Women MPs have struck the bell of fame with a putty hammer.
Cassandra (Sir William Connor) (1909-67), British journalist

A woman is like a teabag – only in hot water do you realise how strong she is.
Nancy Reagan

Women are badly served by writers. It's hopeless for the middle-aged actress. I wasn't going to hang around all my life waiting to play the Nurse in Romeo and Juliet.
Glenda Jackson MP

It is clearly absurd that it would be possible for a woman to qualify as a saint with direct access to the Almighty while she may not qualify as a curate.
Baroness Mary Stocks (1891-1975), British politician, *Still More Commonplace*

To be successful, a woman has to be much better at her job than a man.
Golda Meir

Women's Liberation is just a lot of foolishness. It's the men who are discriminated against. They can't bear children. And no one's likely to do anything about that.
Golda Meir, 1978

Too often the great decisions are originated and given form in bodies made up wholly of men, or so completely dominated by them that whatever of special value women have to offer is shunted aside without expression.
Eleanor Roosevelt, in a speech to the United Nations, 1952

And you're not going to have a society that understands its humanity if you don't have more women in government.
Bella Abzug, US lawyer and congresswoman, *Redbook,* 1974

In politics women . . . type the letters, lick the stamps, distribute the pamphlets and get out the vote. Men get elected.
Clare Boothe Luce, US politician and writer, 1974

Any woman who understands the problems of running a home will be nearer to understanding the problems of running a country.
Margaret Thatcher, 1979

In politics, if you want anything said, ask a man; if you want anything done, ask a woman.
Margaret Thatcher, The Changing Anatomy of Britain, 1982

If all women were enfranchised they would at once swamp the votes of men.
Samuel Evans MP for Glamorgan, Wales, 1906

Whether women are better than men I cannot say
– but I can say they are certainly no worse.
Golda Meir

I've always liked strong women. It doesn't bother
me for people to see her (Hillary) and get excited
and say she could be president. I always say she
could be president too.
Bill Clinton, said during his presidential campaign

Yes . . . very attractive, I never came across any
other woman in politics as sexually attractive in
terms of eyes, wrists and ankles.
Alan Clark, former Defence Minister, when asked during
a television interview if he found Margaret Thatcher
attractive, 1993

No woman in my time will be Prime Minister or
Chancellor or Foreign Secretary – not the top jobs.
Anyway, I wouldn't want to be Prime Minister,
you have to give yourself 100 per cent.
Margaret Thatcher, 1969

A beauty is a woman you notice; a charmer is one
who notices you.
Adlai Stevenson, speech at Radcliffe College, 1963

You are a silly, rude bitch and since you are a
potential breeder, God help the next generation.
Sir Nicholas Fairbairn, Tory MP, to a young woman
heckler

Kinnock is capable, intelligent, forceful, charming,
attractive. Kinnock would make an excellent prime
minister. But we're stuck with her wretched
husband instead.
Anon., Labour MP 1990, of Glenys Kinnock

He is ruled by the person who makes him
breakfast.
Edwina Currie, of Neil Kinnock

I am not prepared to accept the economics of a
housewife.
Jacques Chirac, 1987, of Mrs Thatcher

WORLD POLITICS

AUSTRALIA
Australia is governed by a hierarchy of hicks.
H. B. Turner, 1970

I doubt even the Premier's ability to handle the petty cash box at a hot-dog stall at the local Sunday school picnic.
George Moss, of Sir Henry Bolte, Premier of Victoria, 1969

He does the work of two men – Laurel and Hardy.
Graffiti, of Malcolm Fraser, Prime Minister

He could be described as a cutlery man – he was born with a silver spoon in his mouth and he uses it to stab his colleagues in the back.
Bob Hawke, 1975

CANADA
I did not write S.O.B. on the Rostow document. I didn't think Diefenbaker was a son of a bitch, I thought he was a prick.
John F. Kennedy of John G. Diefenbaker, Prime Minister. Kennedy later defended his words by saying 'I couldn't have called him a S.O.B. – I didn't know he was one at the time'.

The only person I know who can strut sitting down.
John G. Diefenbaker, of Jean Lesage, Premier of Quebec

The greatest thing in political circles since Christine Keeler.
Anon, of Pierre Trudeau, Prime Minister, 1969

In Pierre Elliott Trudeau, Canada has at last produced a political leader worthy of assassination.
Irving Layton, The Whole Bloody Bird, 1969

IRON LADY VERSUS NICE GUY.
TWICE-DIVORCED CHILDLESS WOMAN
AGAINST DEVOTED FAMILY MAN.
Slogans in run-up to Canadian Leadership election between
Kim Campbell and Jean Charest, 1993

She brings a different style. I don't want to be
sexist, but Charest, though young, is from the old
school. He's from Quebec and, well, he's just a
man.
A Campbell supporter from Ontario

Neither of them can beat the Liberals. It's time for
the Tories to take a hike. What Canadians are out
for right now is blood.
A delegate referring to the race between Campbell and
Charest for Canadian leader

He's a man of the people. He's so nice. He's
someone you think you can go up to and hug.
The Globe and Mail, Canadian newspaper, of
candidate Jean Charest

The most important thing is for us to elect the
person who will win this year's general election.
Jean Coreil, Conservative Minister from Quebec, at a
karaoke evening in Charest's honour, 1993

CHILE
Between 3 September and 4 November, Chile is
going to feel like a football being kicked about by
a Pele.
Salvator Gossens Allende, Chilean Socialist Politician
and President, 1970-73 Campaign speech 1970, predicting
the struggle which would follow Socialist victory at the
election

CHINA
The greatest genocidal maniac in the history of the
world, the same Mao Tse-Tung who killed four
times as many Chinese as Hitler killed Jews.
William F. Buckley, Jr, On the Right, 1964

CUBA
As far as I am concerned, Castro is a four
dimensional SOB. An SOB no matter how you
look at him.
Robert Orben, of Fidel Castro

EGYPT
Nasser knew what he did not want, but not quite what he wanted.
Mohammad Heikal, of Gamal Nasser, President

Sadat and Begin remind me of the musical Annie Get Your Gun – anything you can do I can do better.
Yizhak Rabin, of Anwar Sadat, President, 1978

FRANCE
The French will only be united under the threat of danger. How can anyone govern a nation that has 265 different kinds of cheese.
Charles de Gaulle, 1951

Of all the crosses I have to bear, the heaviest is the Cross of Lorraine.
Sir Winston Churchill, of Charles de Gaulle, President

De Gaulle thinks that he is both Joan of Arc and Clemenceau.
Franklin D. Roosevelt

An artless sincere megalomaniac.
H. G. Wells, of Charles de Gaulle, 1943

Le Pen is a bastard and people who vote for him are bastards too.
Bernard Tapie, of Jean Marie Le Pen, 1992

If an atom bomb fell on France he would be there to congratulate himself that there had not been two.
François Giroud, of Valery Giscard D'Estaing, President

Sir, you are in love with yourself. And you don't have a rival on earth.
Napoleon Bonaparte, of Charles Talleyrand, Prime Minister

GERMANY
This bloodthirsty guttersnipe launches his mechanised armies upon new fields of slaughter, pillage and devastation.
Sir Winston Churchill, of Adolf Hitler, 1941

That garrulous monk.
Benito Mussolini, of Hitler

A [horse] racing tipster who only reached Hitler's
level of accuracy would not do well for his clients.
A. J. P. Taylor, historian, of Hitler

A combination of initiative, perfidy, and epilepsy.
Leon Trotsky, of Hitler

INDIA
A seditious Middle Temple lawyer, posing as a
fakir of a type well known in the East.
Sir Winston Churchill, of Mohandas (Mahatma)
Gandhi, 1931

Gandhi has been assassinated. In my humble
opinion a bloody good thing but far too late.
Noel Coward, in his diary, 1948

The so-called leader of the world's largest
democracy struts like a bloated peacock on the
international stage.
Terry Dicks, of Rajiv Gandhi

IRELAND
Politics is the chloroform of the Irish people, or,
rather, the hashish.
Oliver St John Gogarty, 1935

The Spanish onion in the Irish stew.
David Lloyd George, of Eamonn de Valera, Prime
Minister

Mr De Valera is so slippery to deal with it is like
trying to pick up quicksilver with a fork.
David Lloyd George

I do not intend to prejudge the past.
William Whitelaw, on arriving in Ulster as Minister for
Northern Ireland, 1973

I will drive a coach and six horses through the Act
of Settlement
Sir Stephen Rice (1637-1715), English politician

I never met anyone in Ireland who understood the
Irish question, except one Englishman who had
only been there a week.
Major Sir Keith Fraser MP, 1919

Republicans have as much interest in peace as anyone else. It is time for a democratic resolution.
Gerry Adams, Irish politician

When a man takes a farm from which another has been evicted, you must show him by leaving him severely alone, by putting him into a moral Coventry, by isolating him from his kind as if he were a leper of old – you must show him your detestation of the crimes he has committed.
Charles Stewart Parnell (1846-91), Member of Parliament and champion of Irish Home Rule.
The first person to be so treated was a Captain Boycott – hence the verb, to boycott, 1880

Before Irish Home Rule is conceded by the Imperial Parliament, England as the predominant member of the three kingdoms will have to be convinced of its justice and equality.
Lord Rosebery, British statesman, 1894

No man has a right to fix the boundary of the march of a nation; no man has a right to say to his country – thus far shalt thou go and no further.
Charles Stewart Parnell, Irish nationalist politician

ISRAEL
Put three Zionists in a room and they will form four political parties.
Levi Eshkol

He makes Arafat look like a Boy Scout.
Jesse Helms, of Menachem Begin, Prime Minister

He is like a man who steals your cow. You ask for it back and he demands a ransom.
Anwar Sadat, of Menachem Begin

ITALY
It is not impossible to govern Italians. It is merely useless.
Benito Mussolini

A sawdust Caesar.
George Seldes, 1932

JAPAN
The Japanese policy is to make hell while the sun shines.
Sir Winston Churchill

Japan's economic miracle was made possible because the rest of us were ready to keep our markets open to you.
Margaret Thatcher, on the difficulties British companies encounter when trying to do business with Japan, 1989

LIBYA
We are not going to tolerate these attacks from states run by the strangest collections of misfits, loony tunes, and squalid criminals since the advent of the Third Reich.
Ronald Reagan

Not only a barbarian, but flaky.
Ronald Reagan, of Colonel Muammar Gaddafi

Gaddafi is the lunatic of Libya – a dwarf who thought he was a giant.
Anwar Sadat, 1976

MEXICO
Mexico has had 59 revolutions in 63 years, and needs another.
Philadelphia Press

Mexican metric system – Ten bandits make one revolution. Ten revolutions make one government. One government makes ten revolutions.
Boston Transcript

NEW ZEALAND
Lange is the only sixteen stone world leader that can be considered a lightweight.
Anon. Australian MP

The United States has Ronald Reagan, Johnny Cash, Bob Hope and Stevie Wonder. New Zealand has Robert Muldoon, no cash no hope and no bloody wonder.
Graffiti

NICARAGUA
He may be a son of a bitch, but he's our son of a bitch.
Franklin D. Roosevelt, of Anastasio Somozo, President

RUSSIA
The Soviet Union would remain a one-party nation even if an opposition party were permitted – because everyone would join that party.
Ronald Reagan, 1982

The Kremlin is like a baby – it has an appetite one end and no sense of responsibility at the other.
Ronald Reagan

This man has a nice smile, but he's got iron teeth.
Andrei Gromyko, of Mikhail Gorbachev, 1985

A pig-eyed bag of wind.
Frank L. Howley, of Nikita Khrushchev

The Russian's worst misfortune was Lenin's birth; their next worse, his death.
Sir Winston Churchill of Nikolai Lenin

Lenin was an intriguer, a disorganiser and an exploiter of Russian backwardness.
Leon Trotsky

I have never seen a human being who more perfectly represented the modern conception of a robot.
Sir Winston Churchill, of Molotov

Genghis Khan with a telephone.
Anon., of Joseph Stalin, Premier

His abilities seem to consist in vigorous abuse of the people who disagree with him – say ninety-nine out of every hundred in every country and political party in the world.
Lord Birkenhead, of Leon Trotsky

SPAIN
Always I had been afraid that we would come back to power in bad conditions. They could not be worse. Once more we must harvest the wheat when it is still green.
Manuel Dias Azana (1880-1940), Spanish Republican politician on becoming Prime Minister, 1936

SOUTH AFRICA
Sounds more like an avenging angel than a guardian angel.
Anthony Beaumont-Dark, of Nelson Mandela, leader of the ANC

The most potent weapon in the hands of the oppressor is the mind of the oppressed.
Steve Biko (1946-1977), South African Black Nationalist Leader, address to the Cape Town Conference on inter-racial studies, 1971

TURKEY
A man who, though he abhorred political assassination, was not above judicial murder.
Lord Kinross of Kemal Ataturk, President, 1964

He was a dark loquacious character who looked somewhat like Groucho Marx but without the humour.
James Callaghan, of Turan Gunes, Foreign Minister

It was necessary to abolish the fez, which sat on the heads of our nation as an emblem of ignorance, negligence, fanaticism and hatred for progress and civilisation, to accept in its place the hat, the headgear worn by the whole civilised world.
Mustapha Kemal Ataturk (1881-1938), Turkish politician and General President, Speech to the Turkish Assembly, 1927

UGANDA
The African violent.
Bruce B. Randall Jr, of Idi Amin Dada

He is a clown face . . . Satan's buffoon.
Tony Samstag, *The Times,* 1980

The solitary conductor of an orchestra of devils.
Ian Smith, of Idi Amin

INDEX